How to Build

MW01287228

Secrets from a public speaking instructor who has helped others overcome their #1 fear

Erin Lovell Ebanks

Printed in the USA
ISBN: 978-0-9964856-3-0 (paperback)

Happy Professor Publishing books may be purchased for
educational, business, or promotional use. For information on
bulk purchases, please contact Happy Professor Publishing at
Erin@happyprofessor.com.

Cover design: SelfPubBookCovers.com/topcovers

Table of Contents

Introduction

You know.

You don't really have to do this.

You could just drop the class, or tell your sister you won't be able to deliver that speech in her honor on her wedding day, or turn down that six-figure dream job that, by the way, requires you to pitch ideas and present to clients on a regular basis.

But let's be honest.

You're tired of saying "No" to incredible opportunities because you're scared.

You're fed up, and you're ready for a change.

Together, we'll not only face and conquer your fears, but we'll perfect the delivery and the content of your speech as well. Preparing a speech should not be 99% dread and 1% crossing your fingers that you'll be able to get out of it. Preparing a speech should be an exciting time in which you get to develop a unique message in your own voice, and share it with people who are eager to hear it.

~

I've been teaching Public Speaking and various other Communication courses since 2009. Which means I've had hundreds of conversations with (and emails from) students who either have no idea how to get started planning a speech, want me to magically eliminate their fear of public speaking with the wave of a wand, or both.

Wouldn't it be great if both of those problems could be solved with a quick and easy solution?

I've done my best to create YouTube videos (search YouTube.com for the 'Erin Lovell Ebanks Channel'), and long, heartfelt email responses to students to help soothe their fears as much as possible, but none of it seemed to stop the influx of students who wanted answers and solutions in a neat little package.

Then it hit me. I can do that. I can actually work some sort of magic for my students.

It might not be the kind of quick fix you were hoping for, and it most likely won't change your life in the blink of an eye. However, I've packaged up the most valuable tips and tricks regarding public speaking in this book.

Voila!

It's the neat, packaged, 3-step answer to all your public speaking worries.

As someone who has been in your shoes: a former nervous speech student, a scared first-time professor, and a "faking it 'till you make it" presenter (who desperately hoped the beads of nervous sweat weren't showing), I know what you're going through.

I know how frustrated you are that your shaking voice is keeping you from getting your message across in the powerful way that represents you.

I know that you would love to get on stage to showcase that secret talent you have, participate more bravely in class or business discussions, or even just enjoy standing up in front of an audience to present a speech without being completely overwhelmed.

Well, let's get to it!

Step 1 of this book will go over the steps to preparing your speech. Step 2 will help get a handle on your nerves and build confidence. Step 3 will teach you how to actually *enjoy* being in the spotlight.

Lastly, the final portions of this book will leave you with some helpful interviews and resources to use as you continue your public speaking journey.

I'll even share my own personal stories, and those of well-respected speakers who have beat their nerves- not eliminated them- but learned to use that all-too-familiar adrenaline rush to their advantage.

~

First, I thought I'd share some of the biggest concerns that ring true for many new speakers. If you find yourself relating to these, you're not alone! In fact, you're incredibly normal.

If, by the time you finish reading this book, you've taken all the advice and action steps I've given throughout, you can say goodbye to each and every problem listed below.

Good luck on your journey!

Common Concerns for New Speakers (you're not alone!)

(Used anonymously with permission from public speaking students)

"I just want to be able to be myself and not worry about what's going through the minds of my audience members."

"I'd like my future speeches to be perfect, but I realize that may lead to too much pressure and mistakes."

"The element I have the most difficulty with when it comes to public speaking is knowing that all eyes are on me."

"I find that the most difficult element of public speaking is the ability to connect with your audience and stay focused."

"I believe the element that gives me the most difficulty in public speaking is time management. I find myself sometimes having difficulty abiding by certain times limits."

"I think an issue I have with public speaking is a fear of the wrong words coming out of my mouth. My brain can't get the words out properly when I'm in front of a crowd."

"The element of public speaking that gives me the most difficulty is being the center of attention. I have a tendency to be the type of person who would rather just sit back and let someone else get all the attention."

"One would think that since I did theatre and danced most my life, public speaking would come easy, but it's a completely different experience in my opinion, and much more nerve wracking."

~

Now that you've been able to take a look inside the minds of new speakers, hopefully you're feeling some relief knowing that so many people are in the same situation as you.

Let's start learning how to build your message, feel confident, and have fun.

Step 1
<u>Build Your Message</u>

Depending on what you're using as a resource, you're going to get different advice when it comes to speech planning.

The order in which you plan your speech may vary slightly depending on where you look for guidance, and depending on your speaking situation, but the 8 steps we'll talk about can help you with the most basic speeches, as well as the most complex.

In my speech classes, we use the following 8 steps to prepare most speeches:

1. Analyze your audience
2. Develop a topic, specific purpose, thesis statement, and key points
3. Construct a rough-draft outline
4. Conduct research
5. Finalize your organization, introduction and conclusion
6. Make a formal outline and speaking notes
7. Develop purposeful visual aids
8. Rehearse and work out those nerves!

You might look at this list and think, "Wow, that looks kind of boring and basic."

It is basic, but the simplicity works in your favor.

I promise you that each of these steps plays a part in helping you feel more prepared and confident as a speaker. They're all equally important, and will help you take huge steps of progress in the preparation process.

1. Analyze your audience

I once had an online student try to defend her view that 'your speech is just for you,' in a lengthy discussion post.

I very politely corrected her so she wouldn't miss any future quiz questions and/or have the wrong idea for the rest of her life. I've read a lot of speech textbooks over the years, and not one would support the 'speeches are just for the speaker' theory.

That strong opinion of hers was a first for me, and a little off-putting, but I'm glad it happened. Recalling that story always leads to a great discussion in my face-to-face classes.

What do you think? Is there a particular situation where you shouldn't worry about what the audience thinks, and plan the speech just for you? *(If you're reading this book with a group/class, take a minute to discuss your thoughts).*

I can't think of one.

Here's what I'm getting at. If you are about to go through the trouble of planning, organizing, researching, and practicing (a lot) for a speech, you better be very certain it will appeal to your audience. If not, they will have absolutely no problem tuning you out- especially if it's a captive (i.e. classroom) audience, rather than a friendly audience (i.e. a whole audience of paid attendees just dying to hear you speak).

It's so important to analyze your audience that it's the *very* first step in the entire speech preparation process.

Remember, the point of presenting a speech is to teach your audience something, persuade them to do something, challenge their thinking, simply inform them, or entertain them.

How do you plan on doing that if you don't bother to engage them through your message (including words, tone, and body language)?

Jumping a little bit ahead here, when I speak to classes about planning and presenting speeches, I tell them to, of course, analyze the audience demographics and also psychologically analyze the audience.

For example, if you have males and females in the audience, and you're presenting a demonstration speech about how to change a flat tire, you need to include *everyone* who is present. I actually had a female speaker present the above-mentioned speech, and start out with, "This speech is just for the females in the audience."

Do you see what's wrong here? The first line of her speech alienated a good chunk of people who might potentially gain something from her message if she had bothered to appeal to them.

Think about the following topics: breast cancer, hair products, and makeup.

Do males or females come to mind?

Now think about the following topics: cars, video games, and football.

Do males or females come to mind?

If you answered "females" for the first question, and "males" for the second question, that's extremely close-minded of you.

I'm just kidding, that's a natural response from years of living in our society and being surrounded and molded a certain way by the environment (i.e. television, movies, advertising, and even family and peers).

However, it's a very bad idea to exclude the entire male or female portion of your audience. It doesn't mean you can't discuss hair products or cars, it just means you need to be sure you're making it a point to include everybody when it comes to the language you use (i.e. "You women out there might think this doesn't apply to you, but I'm about to change your mind. Keep in mind that women [insert our own inclusive phrase here]").

You'd be amazed at how many student speakers get up in front of the class and say, "For this speech, I'm just going to talk to the _____ in the audience."

(Insert "guys," "women," "procrastinators," "car lovers," "animal lovers," etc. in the space above.)

Discrimination happens to all types of audience members, not just certain races, sexes, or age groups. One time, a student gave a speech that was just for students who wanted to be doctors in the audience (it was a speech about how to apply to medical school, which I think applied to one other student in the class based on all the jargon that was used).

I think you get the point, so I'll wrap up.

Create a speech that will be memorable, enjoyable, and appealing to every single person in your audience. If you don't think you can do that with your topic, either find a new approach or a new topic altogether.

Your Turn
Consider the following for your upcoming speech:

What type of people will be in your potential audience?

What topics have you thought about for your upcoming presentation that would be
appropriate or inappropriate for them?

How can you fix this?

2. Develop a topic, specific purpose, thesis statement, and key points

Now that you've determined what concepts your audience would like to hear about, you can pick a specific topic, but you'll have to do that based on the purpose of your speech.

Here's how to go about determining your purpose:

First, choose one of the following:

Is it a speech to introduce yourself?
Is it a speech to inform?
Is it a speech to persuade?
Is it a speech to entertain?

Good, now that you've picked one, let's get even more specific.

Is it a speech for class? *(In that case, be sure you follow the instructor's rubric very carefully- every teacher will want something different. Take a minute to do that now.)*

Is it a speech for a special occasion? *(If it's for a wedding, funeral, or to accept an award, you most likely won't be citing scholarly sources. Be sure to ask the coordinator of the event, or the person who asked you to speak, what exactly they're looking for time-wise and content-wise. Take a minute to do that now.)*

Now you can go ahead and pick out a topic.

For the sake of keeping the examples to a minimum, let's pretend you're being asked to present an informative speech for your college speech class.

The requirements are:

"Research a topic that will be appealing to your audience and to you as a speaker. You will need to use at least 3 scholarly sources to conduct research for your speech; you will also orally cite these 3 sources during your speech. You must have an introduction, body, and a conclusion. The time limit is 5-7 minutes."

Based on these instructions, it seems that the following might be a bad idea:

A speech about the latest gossip from your favorite reality show
A speech about your childhood years
A speech showing the audience how to make a friendship bracelet

However, you could change the way you approach those topics. If you're truly excited to talk about something related to the above three examples, and you know you can include and engage your entire audience with your particular message, choose a different angle.

The following speeches would be appropriate based on the directions above:

A speech about the history of reality television
A speech about Piaget's Cognitive Stages of Development (Remember to keep it interesting for the audience and don't get too clinical if you're not speaking to Piaget enthusiasts. Use science as well as real life examples, and eliminate any confusing jargon.)
A speech about the history and evolution of friendship bracelets as a hobby that has persisted through time

By approaching your topic differently, you can find a way to give a substantial speech and do some quality research to support your message and build your speaker credibility.

Not interested in reality TV, the adolescent years, or friendship bracelets?

Start brainstorming some different topics that would make your speech preparation and delivery as easy on you as possible.

Don't talk about anything that might become too emotional for you when you present it in front of the class. Choose something you're familiar with, something that you would enjoy talking about, that the audience would enjoy, and don't talk about anything too complex. If you have a 5-7 minute time limit, you'll have to pick the perfect amount of information to share that won't be too basic or too overwhelming.

Your Turn
Consider the following for your upcoming speech:

What are your hobbies?

What do you know a lot about?

What's your favorite class in school?

What are you currently learning about that you find interesting?

What would you like to do as a career?

What are some clubs you've been involved with?

What are some parts of your daily life that you could conduct some research on?

Based on the above questions, I'll start making a list of what topics I could potentially speak about *(Tip: You should do the same!)*:

Your list:

1.
2.
3.
4.
5.

My list:

Guitar
Music
Writing
MacBook Pro
Smart phones
Chia seeds
The history and evolution of candles in America
Education in America
Pets

Have you finished your list yet?

All I did was look around my living room to see what caught my eye, and what I'd be interested in learning more about. It probably took 60 seconds to create the list above.

If I was a student taking a good look at that list, this is how I would narrow down the topics:

I immediately know that I probably don't want to talk too much about the MacBook Pro or smart phones because a lot of groups are split between Apple products and their competitors, and I don't want to feel uncomfortable and even more nervous up in front of the class if all the PC users are going to scowl at me the whole time.

Cross those off if you're a new speaker.

I could talk about writing and its historical beginnings, but my audience might get bored unless I can come up with a really engaging angle, so I think I'll keep looking at the other topics for now and save myself some trouble.

Cross that one off.

Maybe I'll talk about the guitar. I enjoy playing my guitar and watching the performances on the television show *Nashville*, and I've always wanted to go deeper and learn more about the history of the guitar. Many people, especially college students, also seem to be interested in this instrument, so this might be the perfect choice for me and my audience.

Now I'm thinking of a lot more possibilities.

I could choose to speak about:

The history of the city Nashville, Tennessee
Acoustic guitars
Electric guitars
Famous guitarists
Country music

That gives me a good idea! Here we go:

The purpose of my speech is to inform my audience about the different types of guitars.

My three main points will be: acoustic guitar, electric guitar, and slide guitar.

Were you able to follow my thought process? Did it help you through the brainstorming process?

Good!

My three main points could have also been:

The History of Guitars
The Evolution of Guitars
The Future of Guitars

Your Turn
Did you notice I used parallel structure to make the main points
more memorable when I present them to the audience? That means
I used the same grammatical structure for each point for the sake
of readability. Any guesses as to what type of pattern I'd be using
to organize the above-mentioned speech? If you're a speech
student, you should probably familiarize yourself with the different
patterns for the sake of a future quiz grade. The answer is:
chronological pattern.

If I wanted to delve more into acoustic guitars as the topic, rather
than using it as one of the main points, I could use the following
three main points instead:

Acoustic Guitars: The Creation
Acoustic Guitars: The Brands
Acoustic Guitars: The Musicians

Your Turn
Can you tell me what type of structure I used to make the main
points more memorable when I present them to the audience? I'll
give you a hint: it's the same one I used before... Very good! It's a
parallel structure. Any guesses as to what type of pattern I'll be
using to organize this new speech? Again, you might want to
familiarize yourself with the different patterns for the sake of a
future quiz grade. The answer this time is: topical pattern.

At this point, you should have determined your own specific
speech purpose, topic, and three main points.

If you haven't already written them down, do that now.

Let's move on to the next step.

3. Construct a rough-draft outline

Depending on what type of speech you're giving, what type of occasion it will be, and what the requirements are for your speech, the outline you use will vary as you're trying to organize your thoughts.

If you're not sure exactly what main points you're going to stick with yet, draw up several versions with different main points in spots a, b, and c below. There's no harm in testing out different ideas in the beginning stages. Once we get to the research stage, you may find that one version of your rough draft, and one set of main points, turn out to be much easier to research. Then you'll be happy you had a few versions you were playing around with!

Most of the time you can't go wrong with the following basic outline if you're just jotting down some general ideas.

I.   Introduction

II.   Body
    a.   Main Point 1
    b.   Main Point 2
    c.   Main Point 3

III.   Conclusion

Your Turn
Go ahead and jot down a rough outline, or a few rough outlines, using the simple structure below:

I.   Introduction: _____

II.   Body
a.   Main Point 1: _____
b.   Main Point 2: _____

c.   Main Point 3: _____

III.   Conclusion: _____

If you're taking a speech class as a college student, I can almost guarantee your teacher will want to see a rough-draft outline (so she can check your work before you get too deep into the preparation process) that looks a lot like the practice outline below.

Your Turn
Take a minute to complete your own rough draft on notebook paper or in this book. If you did two versions of the more general outline above, this may be the point at which you realize some of your main points don't lend themselves very well to subpoints and supporting information. Maybe they don't qualify to be a main point because of their lack of depth. Completing the outline below will help you determine which areas of your topic deserve to be the main points, and which ones should really just serve as minor supporting details.

Rough-draft outline: Informative Speech

Specific Purpose (not stated verbally as part of your speech):
To inform my audience about _____

Introduction

I. Open with Impact (*Use a quote, shocking statistic, ask the audience a question, or hook them in another way that is appropriate for the audience and speech content*) _____

II. Thesis statement (*State what you'll be speaking about, and why it's of value to your audience members*) _____

III. Preview (*State the three key ideas/main points you'll discuss during the body of your speech*):

A.

_____

B.

_____

C.

_____

Transition statement (*Recap what you just spoke about, and introduce your next main point*) _____

Body

I. Main point (*State what your first main point will be as you begin the body of your speech. For A, B, and C, jot down your subpoints that will be used to support your first main point*)

_____

A.

_____

B.

_____

C.

_____

Transition statement (*Recap what you just spoke about, and introduce your next main point*) _____

II. Main point

_____

A.

_____

B.

_____

C.

_____

Transition statement (*Recap what you just spoke about, and introduce your next main point*) _____

III. Main point

_____

A.

_____

B.

_____

C.

_____

Transition statement (*Recap what you just spoke about, and introduce your conclusion*) _____

Conclusion (*Sum up your three main points. Then for parts A, B, and C, restate the three main ideas or three key 'takeaways' from your speech.*)

I. Sum up your speech _____

A.

_____

B.

_____

C.

_____

II. Close with Impact (*Choose a closing that refers back to your opening and wraps up your speech nicely, using a quote, something you want them to remember, a call to action, etc. You want the closing to be meaningful.*)

_____

References (*If the rough-draft outline is for your eyes only, or to share with a few close friends, there is no need to list your references at this point unless you might forget where you found some key information. If your rough draft is for a class, your teacher may or may not ask you to include your references here as part of the assignment. The number of sources required or suggested will vary depending on the type of speech, the circumstances surrounding the speech, and the person inviting you to give the speech.*)

1. _____
2. _____
3. _____

4. Conduct research

Once you have your main points and subpoints organized, you'll have a better idea of what areas you'll need to research.

One mistake I see with students is that they spend countless hours researching their broad topic when they haven't picked out the specific areas they'll want to speak about (this is why developing a rough draft is so important before you start your research).

This can be frustrating, and a waste a of precious time, so be sure you know the key points you need to research before you dive in, and keep the time requirements in mind. Thirty hours of research for a 5-7 minute speech is probably way too much time!

On the other hand, if you're giving an hour-long presentation, you may want to incorporate research, personal anecdotes, some audience participation, and a lot of energy to keep your audience actively engaged for the entire 60 minutes. There will be a lot less involvement in a typical 5-7 minute presentation required for speech class, commencement addresses, and general special occasion speeches (that may come your way when you least expect it).

Once you know exactly what specifics you'll want to research, be sure to use credible sources that your audience will trust and respect. There's nothing worse than hurting your credibility with websites that aren't conventionally known to be trustworthy. You want the audience to respect you and like you.

You can use the CRAAP test to be sure you're on the right track:

Currency- the information should be current
Relevance- the information should relate to your topic
Authority- the author's/source's credentials should qualify them to write about the topic
Accuracy- the information should be correct
Purpose- the information should be objective and unbiased

*(If you're not sure where to start, I usually suggest Google
Scholar: scholar.google.com.)*

It's also okay to discuss your own experiences as part of a speech;
it builds your credibility as you prove to the audience that you have
a history with the topic, and it keeps your audience's interest.
However, depending on the speech, you may need additional
credible sources and specific content that might enhance your
speech (i.e. facts, stats, expert opinion, etc.) as well.

Remember not to overdo the statistics or personal stories, a balance
of the two is a great way to have a memorable and impressive
speech.

Your Turn
Consider the following for your upcoming speech:

What type of speech will I be giving?

Will it require research?

How many credible sources will I need to include?

What type of research would add to my credibility as a speaker?

*Where can I look in the library and online to find the best
information on my topic?*

*Make a list of 5 potential books, magazine, journals, and/or
websites in which you could find some quality research material:*

1.
2.
3.
4.
5.

Now make a list of 5 specific articles you've decided on. Use MLA or APA format to add them below. Go to easybib.com, citationmachine.com, or another bibliography generator to guide you through completing this step:

1.
2.
3.
4.
5.

5. Finalize your organization, introduction and conclusion

There are a few ways to organize your points.

Chronological Pattern- main points are arranged in order of date or by steps
Causal Pattern- main points are arranged either by effect, then cause, or cause, then effect
Topical or Claim Pattern- main points are arranged by category
Geographic or Spatial Pattern- main points are arranged according to location

(I won't discuss each of these in depth, for the sake of maintaining the integrity of our "neat, packaged, 3-step" book.)

There is not necessarily a right or wrong way to organize your points; it depends on the way you want to approach the topic. However, once you pick an organizational pattern, there *is* a right or wrong way to organize it. For instance, if you're giving us step-by-step directions for brushing our teeth (i.e. a chronological pattern), we don't want to put the toothbrush in our mouth and start scrubbing before we've added the toothpaste.

Most of the time, especially for informative speeches, my students choose to use the **topical pattern**. For instance, they might break down a speech about different fruits by discussing bananas, apples, and then oranges. It doesn't really matter where each of those main points goes; they're simply organized by category. You might start noticing that many speeches are designed using the topical pattern.

Causal pattern (not "casual" pattern, to be used for casual topics; I've had a surprising number of students make that assumption) is another one to look at more closely. If you're giving a speech to inform, you should be careful here so it doesn't become a persuasive speech, which might rub your audience or your teacher the wrong way.

One of the most important things in developing and presenting a speech is keeping in mind what the purpose of your speech is (to inform? persuade? entertain?). If you fail to do what you were asked to by a boss, client, or a teacher, it can be an embarrassing experience. Most of the time, persuasive speeches are organized with cause first, followed by effect. In informative speeches, cause can be followed by effect, or effect can be followed by cause. Either way is fine.

Don't spend a significant amount of time determining the *type* of organization you plan to use, but *do* spend plenty of time ensuring that your speech has the correct ideas and components in the right places for the most effective speech.

Your Turn
Consider the following for your upcoming speech:

What type of speech will I be giving?

Will the purpose be to inform, persuade, or entertain?

What type of organization would be most appropriate?

Does the organization of my speech match the purpose of my speech?

~

I'm not sure why, but planning the introduction and conclusion are some of my favorite steps to discuss in speech class.

It might seem strange that planning the very beginning of your speech comes so close to the end of the preparation process, but once you understand the reasoning, it'll make perfect sense.

Keynote speakers, public speaking coaches, and especially public speaking instructors are very big on emphasizing the importance of making sure your speech is as effective as it can possibly be. This includes ensuring that your speech makes sense from beginning to end.

Think about it. When you're initially preparing your speech, you're probably tempted to jot down an idea for a really great opening and closing (that have an impact and really tie the speech together nicely, of course).

However, how many times did you change some of the ideas surrounding your speech topic as you were scribbling down some rough main points? Not only that, but how many times did you end up changing your main points and subpoints altogether?

Do your premature introduction and conclusion still make sense when presented with your changed speech content?

(By the way, this is why you may want to have a few sheets of paper, or a pencil with an eraser, handy as you are working on your rough draft. Things will change!)

It's always surprising when a speaker has a great speech, but the ending falls flat because it failed to wrap up the speech in a way that made sense.

This is also why you should wait until just before you prepare your speaking notes to develop your introduction with a really fantastic attention-getter, that not only hooks your audience, but is also applicable to your speech content, and ties nicely to your impactful closing.

In addition, you want to be sure as you near the end of your speech preparation, that your purpose and thesis statement are still appropriate for the body of your speech, and that the preview of your main points leading into the speech have stayed the same through the entire process.

It's not just students that have to be careful about planning their introduction and conclusion. On occasion, professional speakers can fail to complete this step when they're excited to get to the rehearsal stage of their speech.

Remember, the attention-getter, thesis statement, preview, and conclusion should all make sense as a group, and should accurately give an insight into the main points and body of your speech.

Your Turn
Consider the following for your upcoming speech, while looking at your rough-draft outline:

What are the main points, subpoints, and supporting information in my speech?

What would be the most effective **introduction** *for this particular audience, type of speech, and content? (Intro= Attention-getter, Thesis statement, and Preview)*

What would be the most effective **conclusion** *that would wrap up my speech while connecting well with my attention-getter? (Conclusion= Sum up your speech, Restate key ideas, and Close with Impact)*

Be sure that your attention-getter and closing statement have impact!

Fill in the following introduction and conclusion with your ideas for your upcoming speech:

Introduction

Specific Purpose (not stated verbally as part of your speech):
To inform my audience about _____

I. Open with Impact (*Use a quote, shocking statistic, ask the audience a question, or hook them in another way that is appropriate for the audience and speech content*) _____

II. Thesis statement (*State what you'll be speaking about, and why it's of value to my audience members*) _____

III. Preview (*State the three key ideas/main points you'll discuss during the body of your speech*):

A.

_____

B.

_____

C.

_____

Conclusion

(*Sum up your three main points. Then for parts A, B, and C, restate the three main ideas or three key 'takeaways' from your speech.*)

I. Sum up your speech _____

A.

_____

B.

_____

C.

_____

II. Close with Impact (*Choose a closing that refers back to your opening and wraps up your speech nicely, using a quote, something you want them to remember, a call to action, etc. You want the closing to be meaningful.*) _____

6. Make a formal outline and speaking notes

After creating a rough-draft outline, doing research, organizing your main points, and deciding on an official introduction and conclusion, you're going to create one last outline, and then you're almost done!

A formal outline is an extended version of your rough-draft outline, but you should not use your formal outline when you're on stage giving your speech (that's what your speaking notes are for). The formal outline is to be used only as part of the planning process.

In some classrooms, another name for the formal outline is a 'preparation outline.' If you are currently a speech student, this term might ring a bell.

The formal outline, or preparation outline, is used to help you organize your thoughts toward the end of the speech preparation process. It should help you determine if something is out of place, if one main point doesn't have enough much-needed research behind it, or if it looks like main point number one is completely taking over the body of your speech (maybe it has a lot more supporting information than your other two main points).

It also makes it much easier for friends, colleagues, and teachers to review your speech (without having to read an entire manuscript) if you would like some feedback.

One of the most important points here is that a formal outline helps you maintain the extemporaneous nature of your speech.

Even though you won't actually be taking your formal outline up on stage with you, writing an initial manuscript may tempt you to eventually read your speech word for word to your audience. Remember, your goal is to be a more conversational and connected speaker, so avoid the temptation of using a manuscript at all cost.

Yes, manuscript speeches (i.e. graduation ceremonies), memorized speeches (i.e. a monologue for a play, and professional keynote speeches), and impromptu speeches (i.e. someone asks you to give an unexpected toast at a celebration dinner) are all appropriate in certain situations, but extemporaneous speeches are the accepted style in many settings today.

Think about the college classroom, meetings with clients, TED talks (yes, they have monitors on the floor to help guide them if you never noticed; it's easy to miss that detail!), and workshops by those who present for a living.

What's the one characteristic those deliveries all have in common?

They're extemporaneous, meaning they are prepared and delivered with as much effort as manuscript speeches delivered from a lectern, but there is still enough wiggle-room for slight changes during the final presentation, and a more natural connection with the audience.

So just remember, a formal/preparation outline is the best way to help you *prepare* to give the best speech.

Your Turn
Develop your formal outline using the following example. Type your outline on a personal computer and don't forget to save it, back it up, and print it.

Notice that this outline is written in full sentences, with full sentence transitions between main points, and a complete list of references at the end (depending on the speaking situation, you may need to include slightly more or slightly less information).

Informative Speech Formal Outline
ASD

Topic: Autism Spectrum Disorder (ASD)

Opening with Impact:

Raise your hands if you know someone with Autism or if you know the parents of an Autistic child. Most of you probably don't know that there are really three types of Autism categorized under the Autism Spectrum Disorder or ASD for short. That's what I'll tell you about today, and you'll see that it's probably more common than you think.

Audience Connection and Speaker Credibility = Statistic Slide:

According to the Centers for Disease Control and Prevention, 11 in every 1000 children in the United States have been diagnosed with ASD since 2008. That breaks down to about 1 in every 100 children. To understand that number a little bit more, it means that in the 3 or 4 classes each of you take in a normal semester; one person in those classes represents someone who could have ASD. That's pretty common in my opinion.

Thesis Statement:

Today I'll give you a little bit more information about ASD, and by the end of my speech you'll know more about this condition and you'll be able to understand the differences between the 3 types of ASD. You'll also be given valuable information that will help you understand what it's like to have a child diagnosed with ASD.

Preview of Main Points:

- Autism
- Asperger syndrome
- Pervasive developmental disorder

4 Transitions: (I will use movement and language after preview and each main point,) "I have just informed you about...now I will be moving to my next main point Autism"
(Transition: Now that I've given you an idea of what I'll be speaking about today, I'll give you some basic information about autism.)

Body and Supporting Material = Main Points, subpoints, research

- Autism
  o Definition – Developmental disorder characterized by impaired communication.
  o Symptoms – Doesn't hold eye contact, imitate facial expressions, or respond to his or her name.
  o The individual – Needs help throughout life.

(Transition: Now that you have a good idea of what autism is, I'll tell you about another type of ASD: Asperger's syndrome.)

- Asperger's syndrome
  o Definition – Developmental disorder characterized by impaired social skills.
  o Symptoms – Doesn't pick up on social cues, avoids eye contact or stares.
  o The individual – Focus on one or few sets of interests.

(Transition: Now that you know about high functioning autism, or Asperger syndrome, I'll tell you about pervasive developmental disorder.)

- Pervasive developmental disorder
  o Definition – Any disorder in the development of the basic psychological functions.
  o Symptoms – Problems with communication and play.

- o The individual – Almost entirely functional in society.

(Transition: After hearing about the different disorders that make up ASD, I'll move on to my summary.)

Conclusion = Summary of important facts reviewed during main points of the speech

- Autism is part of a larger disorder called Autism Spectrum Disorder
- Asperger is a less severe case of autism, where verbal communication is not a problem
- Pervasive developmental disorder is the diagnosis when children don't fit into the two other categories of ASD

Clincher/ End statement: So the next time you hear someone talk about autism, or you hear it mentioned on TV, hopefully you'll have your facts straight and you'll understand that there's more to it than meets the eye.

Research of Credible Sources:

Asperger's syndrome (2012). Retrieved June 14, 2012 from http://www.mayoclinic.com/health/aspergers-syndrome/DS00551

Centers for Disease Control and Prevention (2008). Retrieved June 13, 2012 from www.cdc.gov.

Charman, T., Baron-Cohen, S., Swettenham, J., Baird, G., Drew, A., and Cox, A. (2003). Predicting language outcome in infants with autism and pervasive developmental disorder. International Journal of Language and Communication Disorders, 38 (3), 265-285.

Singh, J. et al. (2009). Trends in US Autism Research Funding. *Journal of Autism Developmental Disorder*, 39, 788-795

What is Autism? What Causes Autism? (2012). Retrieved June 13, 2012 from www.medicalnewstoday.com/info/autism.

~

The final outline/final notes you create will be your speaking notes.

These will be brief, may be highlighted and underlined in certain areas, and will include notes to yourself in the margins, such as "Breath" or "Slow down," if you normally have an issue in those areas. Some people even add, "You're doing great!" to keep up their confidence throughout the speech. These notes are just for you as you present to a crowd (although some speech instructors may ask to see them before or after you present).

The most effective speaking notes would likely be written on 3x5-inch note cards.

Your Turn
Develop your speaking notes using the following example. Write your speaking notes on 3x5-inch note cards.

*Below is an example of a manuscript, followed by the most important part, some brief **speaking notes** for an in-class introduction speech, in which students tell a personal story for 2-4 minutes.*

Note: I wrote out the following manuscript/outline below so my students could see what the content and manuscript of an introduction speech might look like, as well as to get them used to seeing something in outline format:

Introduction Speech Manuscript/Outline Example

Title: My Life as a Procrastinator

I. Introduction
A. Open with an impact statement (Question, visualization, quote, etc.)
("How many of you procrastinated when it came to preparing your speech today?")

B. Basic information about yourself that will help transition to the body of your speech
("Thank you for your honesty! My name is Bob Smith, I'm a first year Business major here at Seminole, and today I'm going to tell you about my life as a procrastinator.")

II. Body

A. Start/ tell your story (you can make the entire body of your speech/story one main point, or split it up as 2 or 3 main points, I'll leave that up to you)

1. History
("You see, when I was a junior in high school, the procrastination started. School got a little harder that year, and I didn't really know how to handle it, so I started to avoid doing homework until the morning it was due, which really stressed me out. To make things worse, I would study for huge exams the night before a test, starting at midnight, which meant I would skip sleeping for the night, go straight into my test, and usually forget about half of it.")

2. Evolution
("My problem started to get worse in my senior year, and I was getting no sleep, always trying to catch up on the homework I should have done when it was assigned earlier- and of course I was trying to pull all-nighters every time I had a test. I started getting really bad grades, mostly D's. The worst time was when I actually fell asleep for part of a 100 question multiple choice test in my

English class, and woke up after everyone had already left class. I was left all alone- except for the teacher- I was embarrassed, and I only answered about 10 questions before I dozed off, so I definitely got an F and knew there was no way I could get above a D in that class. I was pretty disappointed in myself, so that's when I knew I needed to change my ways.")

3. How I changed it
("After that horrible experience, which happened during the first month of my senior year of high school, I started going to the local library right after school for just two hours to get whatever work I was assigned, done. I really hated it at first, but I told myself I just had to stay for two hours and then I could leave. It ended up taking so much pressure off me to have stuff done early on, and sometimes I would stay for a few extra minutes or an extra hour or so. It didn't require too much dedication, just 2 to 3 uninterrupted hours every day- with my cell phone turned off- and I felt drastically different. I felt responsible, I wasn't sleep deprived anymore, I was more relaxed, and I didn't dread going to class anymore. I ended up getting all A's and B's that semester, except for that one "D" I mentioned earlier. That whole journey really taught me that it doesn't pay to procrastinate, and school didn't have to be as bad as I had made it out to be."

III. Conclusion

A. Wrap up statement- keep it short and sweet
("So now that you've all heard my story, hopefully you've learned more about me, and you won't plan any all night cram sessions this semester. Thank you.")

Speaking notes based on the above manuscript:

Notice that the entire introduction and entire conclusion are written out on the first and last note cards. These are the only parts of your speech that should be written out in full as you present your speech.

Introduction Speech: Speaking Notes

Note Card 1

(Introduction)
-How many of you procrastinated when it came to preparing your speech today?
- My name is Joe Brown, I'm a first year Business major here at Seminole.
- Today I'm going to tell you about my life as a procrastinator.

Note Card 2

(Main Point 1. History)
-My history with procrastination
-Examples: started junior year, homework in the morning, all night studying

Note Card 3

(Main Point 2. Evolution)
-How my procrastinating evolved throughout junior and senior year
-Examples: senior year, getting bad grades, asleep during test = F and embarrassed
- Decided to change

Note Card 4

(Main Point 3. How I changed my ways)
-What I did to do homework and study ahead of time
-Examples: 2 hours in lib every day, felt responsible & less stressed, good grades as a result

Note Card 5

(Conclusion)
So now that you've all heard my story, hopefully you've learned more about me, and you won't plan any all night cram sessions this semester.
Thank you.

~

Note/Confession:

This is not an attempt to undo all the good I've done in helping you prepare the various outlines for your speech, but I went from a scared student speaker, to a less scared speaking instructor, and finally to a confident speaking instructor, so I think my personal experience here might be of value.

Clearly, something about my approach as a student speaker worked in my favor, so I want to share some details and insights about my own public speaking journey with you.

Different public speaking resources may give you different advice for writing and preparing the content of your speech, so be sure to follow the style your instructor, or coordinator of the event, expects from you.

I'll confess, as a student, I had a completely different style of preparing. I'll share it with you in the hopes that it might help lead you to (eventually) follow the correct steps for an extemporaneous delivery.

I *did* type out my speeches word-for-word, against the advice of my speech instructors, the moment the ideas started flowing in my college dorm room. This happened almost immediately after the speech had been assigned. In my mind, I had to get started, otherwise the anxiety would start to take its toll.

After I had written my thoughts, I would read from the computer screen out loud, start making changes and additions, and start reading aloud again as if I was speaking in front of a crowd (but from my desk chair). I would continue this pattern for about an hour.

I would then print what I had written (double spaced in Arial 24-ish point font, so it would be easy to read, as well as aid in eye contact without losing my place), and stand up with the printed pages. I would use hand gestures and a conversational speaking tone as I proceeded to read. Here and there I would scratch things out when they sounded too formal as I verbalized them. I added more casual language in the margins, and drew arrows when one paragraph would have made better sense later in the speech.

I did all of this repeatedly until I could read the manuscript, plus my additions and changes, with some eye contact for my fake audience. Eventually, I could read it in a way that felt conversational, well-organized, and true to my own speaking voice.

I'm not quite done yet (I took a very long time to prepare speeches as a student, and I still do. There's no shame in that if you can relate!).

I would then cut out parts of the speech from the printed pages and tape them to the index cards in order to get the right feel for the actual speech day.

I wrote down the words "Breathe here" in parts of the speech where I felt it might appear more natural to my audience to take a breath than in other areas. (Keep in mind that it is okay to breathe more often throughout your speech. However, I was convinced that the audience would be taking note of my every breath and nervous fumble, so I was especially careful.)

I also knew I would probably have a hard time breathing altogether when giving my final speech. I figured it would be best to plan that out ahead of time, and it was.

After repeating the speech out loud, over and over again, and after it had taken many forms and shapes (verbally and physically), I would highlight different key phrases and words:
1. Those that were my main points and subpoints
2. Those that I knew would jog my memory for the next 30 seconds of verbal content, so I could have an easier time maintaining eye contact
3. Third, and probably most importantly, those that I kept forgetting

After practicing with these new and improved, highlighted, makeshift note cards for a day or so, I would transfer only the highlighted parts (in actual writing) to brand new note cards.

I practiced with these new note cards (the proper note cards that most speech textbooks recommend) for the remaining days before my presentation, in front of my roommate, friends, and even on speakerphone with family members.

I practiced in front of various audiences, at different times, and in different settings, too. It wasn't fun, it was very scary, but I always felt invincible after each practice session, and you can't beat that feeling of confidence.

I practiced in front of a number of different small groups to get used to my nerves, figure out how to think on my feet during brief moments of forgetfulness, and build up my confidence for the final presentation day.

Then on the day of the actual speech, I would keep practicing.

Once in the classroom, my classmates would confide in me that they were nervous and should have prepared more. I always lied and said, "I feel pretty good."

And you know what?

After saying that to a few people, every time speech day came around, and realizing that I had been dubbed the most prepared and confident person in the room (every time), I started to *really* feel that way.

I had officially "faked it 'til I made it."

Not only did I feel ready, and proud to present, but I was able to present in a dynamic, connected way with the audience.

My classmates always thought I was a natural, but nobody knew what had really gone on behind the scenes.

~

I didn't tell you this story to convince you to throw out your preparation notes or speaker notes, and secretly write a manuscript instead. I wanted to share this with you so you can start preparing in the way that benefits you and your audience the most.

Everyone is different.

Search for advice in books, online, and from friends and teachers. Ultimately, though, you should prepare in a way that allows for *your* best extemporaneous presentation to deliver a valuable, quality message to your audience in a way that keeps them engaged and connected.

And of course, in a way that will leave you feeling invincible.

*(Keep in mind, if you're a professional speaker preparing a **keynote speech** that you'll likely practice around a hundred times before presenting to your first big audience, and you may commit every word to memory. Every keynote speaker is different, but it will likely be more appropriate for a speech to be memorized in your specific situation.)*

7. Develop purposeful visual aids

Having some purposeful visual aids in your presentation can enhance your message. It's worth learning about, since much of the time it's required, whether by your boss or instructor.

Some helpful visual aids include flip charts, posters, physical objects, overhead transparencies, PowerPoint, Keynote, Prezi, Google Slides, etc. The last two in that list have become popular during the last 5 years (at least in my classrooms), and with the constant advances in presentation technology, I wouldn't be surprised if there were one or two more available for your use by the time you read this book.

Here are a few tips when developing your visual aids (most likely you'll be asked to use a PowerPoint or similar program to present your speech):

- You should be the main focus as the speaker, not your visual aid, so keep the pictures and text minimal and purposeful.
- Roughly follow the 6x6 rule (maximum of six lines of text per slide, and maximum of six words per line)
- Don't overdo it with the slides. One slide for every one or two minutes of your presentation is fine, or you can have even fewer slides.
- Your font should be big enough for the audience to read. In a classroom, a minimum of 24-point font is fine. However, if you're going to be in a huge auditorium, visit a room that's similar in size ahead of time, project your slides, stand in the back, and see if it looks appropriate.
- Use simple fonts
- Don't use full sentences
- Capitalize the first letter of the word that comes immediately after the bullet point (like I've been doing here)

- Test out the colors ahead of time to be sure they're easy to see (many of the colors look different on your laptop than they do on a projector).
- Avoid the animation feature in PowerPoint. There's no reason your audience should have to watch your last line of text swirl around in a circle, or have to hear a car speed by every time you click to the next slide. If you're desperate for animation, the "appear" feature is normally acceptable in professional settings.

Here are a few tips when presenting with visual aids:

- If you plan to use the "clicker" (also known as the presentation remote control), be sure the batteries work in the one provided, bring your own instead, or designate someone to help you control the slideshow as you speak. This way you can still have room to move around without being limited to the podium area.
- Avoid reading directly from your slides.
- Don't turn your back to the audience when looking for keywords on your slide.
- Gesture to visuals and important points on your slides using the hand closest to the projected screen, that way you remain facing the audience while you guide them.
- You can move away from the projected screen. There's no need to feel chained to the wall where your presentation is. Feel free to roam closer to the audience to increase your immediacy (connectedness between you and them).

Lastly, just as some people might spend far too much time researching material for a short speech that should not require much research, people also spend sleepless nights making the most impressive PowerPoint presentation.

Your visual aids should be a helper and a guide for your audience, but it should only be a small part of your speech, and should never become a distraction.

Your Turn
Consider the following for your upcoming speech:

Should I use a visual aid in my speech? (Ask the coordinator of the event, your boss, or teacher what's expected of you)

What type of visual aid should I use?

What content and visuals will I put on each slide?

Now create your visual presentation using the program of your choice.

8. Rehearse and work out those nerves!

This is the time to put all that research, organization, and careful planning to the test!

It's easy to get caught up in the preparation that needs to happen while you are approaching your speech day, but it is just as important to put as much time into practicing your delivery.

I have had countless students prepare a well-thought out, well-researched, and organized speech, only to get up at the front of the room to read from their note cards, speak softly in a monotone voice, and never make a single hand gesture.

If the speech had been a written paper, it would have been easy to give it an A. However, a public speaking class is about public speaking, not public reading.

When you're giving a presentation for school or work, you must connect with your audience, be dynamic and engaging, and show that you have the professional skills of a well-prepared presenter. That includes spending just as much time preparing your delivery as you did preparing your content.

Practicing your delivery with your visual aids (preferably in the room you will be giving the actual presentation in), especially with a small audience present, will not only help you with your presentation skills, but you will be making small steps toward a more confident final presentation.

On the day of your speech, get to the room early and get your presentation set up on the computer. Be sure everything is working accordingly, that your slides are projecting properly, and that the audience can hear you from the stage. Test the equipment to be sure the presentation remote control is working and that you are comfortable with it, and be sure the volume is at an appropriate level in case you were planning on showing a video clip. Be sure you're able to access any audio or video clips you plan to include, as well.

Lastly, talk with some of the audience members. If they happen to be your classmates, engage in small talk about each other's classes, or talk about your speech topics and why you decided on them.

If you were invited to speak at an event, whether to deliver a keynote address or to give the best man speech at a wedding, talk with those in attendance in the minutes leading up to your presentation. Ask them where they're from, ask what they expect from the event, and ask what their favorite moment has been so far.

Not only will those audience members be more invested in listening to you when you start presenting, but they are also more likely to smile at you. If you feel comfortable, and it's appropriate, bring bits of your conversation with them into certain parts of your speech. It will make the entire audience feel more connected to your message since you have made a clear effort to verbally involve them.

Tips to remember:

- It's okay to use purposeful movement and/or gestures, but don't overdo it.
- Maintain quality eye contact with a few friendly faces in the audiences.
- Speak slowly and articulately so you are easy to understand
- Speak at an appropriate volume
- Smile, and laugh with your audience
- Remain energized regardless of the way your audience is responding. It might take them a while to come around, but they will. It's up to you to win them over!
- Avoiding acknowledging how nervous you are, what aspects of the technology are disappointing you, and any slides/portions of your speech that are missing. No one will notice if you don't mention it!

We'll get more into how to practice your speech and build confidence in the next section.

Your Turn
To rehearse for your upcoming speech (this is the way I would do it, but you can make adjustments to suit your own personal style):

1. Practice your presentation with your speaker notes out loud by yourself until you're comfortable.

2. Practice with your notes in front of a mirror until you're comfortable.

3. Practice your presentation while recording yourself. After watching the video, make whatever adjustments are necessary, then record yourself until you're comfortable with the way the presentation looks and sounds.

4. Call a friend/family member and put them on speakerphone to present.

5. Present in front of one person.

6. Present in front of three people.

And so on. Over and over again, with an ever increasing number of willing friends and family members, until you're confident about your speech.

~

I'm just checking in!

Now that you've completed the last step, and have spoken your message out loud in full at least once, you might be surprised that each step paid off so much. It's natural to look at the 8-step list initially and think, "This doesn't look exciting."

However, after having used the process once, it's easy to see how much help it can potentially be in the future.

As a speech instructor and as a human with social connections (like all of you!), inevitably I've been asked to give speeches at family events, and I've taken it upon myself to develop new lectures from time to time.

It always makes me laugh when I have to start the 8-step-process for myself. I usually start by thinking about who my audience is, what my topic will be, and then I think, "Oh no, where do I go from here?"

It's natural as a human to be overwhelmed at the prospect of not just presenting a speech, but taking the steps to prepare it appropriately.

Luckily, right after the, "Oh no, where do I go from here?" moment, I remember that I'm a public speaking instructor and the inner workings of preparing a speech (that you now have access to) have been ingrained in me over years of repetition.

With a little bit of practice, these steps will become second nature to you, too.

So the next time someone approaches you to give a speech for an upcoming special occasion, or to present a talk as a member of a club, you'll know where to go from there!

Step 2
Feel Confident

We've all heard it before: People fear public speaking more than death itself.

Jerry Seinfeld has famously made jokes about people generally preferring to be the one in the coffin rather than the guy delivering the eulogy.

Aren't we tired of this being true?

The fear of speaking to a crowd prevents many people from getting ahead in life. As a public speaking instructor myself, I like to think I'm immune to this condition that afflicts so many of us. However, as many teachers will admit, we are much more comfortable in our own classrooms, and tend to be quite nervous speaking in different settings.

However, the key is to understand that overcoming your fear of public speaking requires constantly performing outside your comfort zone, in a new room, with new people, and new material, in order to continually grow as a performer. You also need to have an understanding of yourself and how you operate to feel your best on presentation day.

The best way to do that is by following the 4 steps we will cover in this section:

1. Prepare and practice
2. Understand and control your unique anxiety
3. Try different techniques for increasing confidence
4. Frame your anxiety differently

1. Prepare and practice

You can read every book possible that shares helpful techniques for overcoming speaking nerves, but here are the two biggest tricks I have found that will work each time for every person (unless you suffer from extremely high communication apprehension, in which case, you should seek out specific help for your situation):

Prepare your material as best you can with plenty of time to practice. Most importantly, practice out loud and in front of people a lot.

That's it. Sounds too easy, right? Would you actually take the initiative to do it?

If you hesitated, and eventually mumbled a, "Maybe," that's where the problem comes in with most people and students.

If you have a problem with procrastination (most of my students claim this is their main problem), keep this in mind:

You will feel your calmest and most confident about your upcoming speech while you are preparing for said speech.

If you have a hard time believing me, give it a shot. I can always tell which students of mine feel most apprehensive about giving a speech, yet will likely feel very comfortable during their presentation (hence having one of the best speeches in the class), because they are the students who have a speech topic and some questions ready to ask me about their organization about 5 minutes after I have assigned the speech.

If you're starting to get the impression that everyone gets nervous at one time or another, you're right. If you think you will be the only nervous speaker on speech day, you are very wrong. Every other speaker will also be nervous.

I'm 100% certain about that.

Being nervous is completely natural. It means that you care about doing a good job, and the added energy/adrenaline even helps you to give a better speech than you would give otherwise.

The problem is when you fail to use that nervous/excited energy boost to your advantage. Some people allow it to sabotage their preparation and final delivery, while others decide to make lemonade out of lemons.

The latter works beautifully.

I'll describe two different scenarios for you:

Scenario 1

Bob is very nervous about his speech. As soon as the instructor announces that a speech will be due in two weeks, his heart starts pounding.

He doesn't want to think about it. He comes up with a few different topics, but has a hard time settling on one, so he starts avoiding it altogether. He avoids talking to anyone about his hesitation and uncertainty (definitely not the teacher), he keeps the anxiety to himself, and fills those two weeks with other distractions.

The night before the speech is due, he quickly and uncomfortably writes out his speech. He's not actually that crazy about the topic, and he's not that familiar with it, which makes his stomach lurch a little bit at this new uncomfortable thought.

"Oh well, it's too late now," he thinks.

On the day of his speech, on three hours of sleep, he rushes in to class and practices his presentation in his head a few times before the instructor calls him up to present.

He does not feel confident, and he's mad at himself for procrastinating again. To make matters worse, Bob has no interest in this topic. He doesn't know the content well enough, and he stumbles over his words.

The audience appears to be put-off by his lack of preparation, and they are uninterested in his topic, due to his clear lack of enthusiasm.

After taking his seat, Bob decides he will get through this semester, but he hates public speaking. He's decided it's too scary and complicated, so he plans to try to avoid it for the rest of his life.

(Have you ever been in Bob's shoes before? I promise you it's not too late to have a much more positive experience as a speaker. See Scenario 2.)

Scenario 2

Sue is very nervous about her speech. As soon as the instructor announces that a speech will be due in two weeks, her heart starts pounding.

She doesn't want to think about it, but she knows that if she puts off the assignment, it will only make her feel worse. She comes up with a few different topics, but she has a hard time settling on one. She decides to talk to her instructor and then with her friends, who help her narrow it down to a topic she feels comfortable with, enthusiastic about, and well-versed in.

She still feels nervous even though she has prepared her content well ahead of time. So she talks to her friends and teacher about it, and decides to confront her feelings head on. She knows that if she bottles it all up, and tries to ignore her feelings about the upcoming speech, it will only lead to a bad situation.

Already feeling good about having prepared her content, she spends the next few days practicing her delivery out loud in front of the mirror, and making tweaks until she feels confident enough to record herself presenting alone.

After watching her recordings, and realizing she needs to be careful not to play with her hair and to be sure to talk more enthusiastically rather than in a soft, timid tone of voice (both things she had no idea she was doing!), she decides to record herself a few more times. She is much happier with the outcome, and surprised by how professional and confident she seems when playing it back.

Sue decides it's time to practice for other people.

She practices four times for her three roommates. She gives them the grading form her teacher will be using, so they can give her valuable feedback.

She felt nervous while presenting for her roommates, and realizes she needs to breathe more while she speaks. She adds that note to a few of her note cards after a practice presentation: "Breathe here."

She's having a hard time scheduling a practice session with some of her other friends, so one day before class starts, she arrives early and asks the teacher if she can practice in the classroom to get a feel for things.

A few students are present, but they cheer her on as she gets ready to practice.

Once again, a new set of nerves hit Sue, but she already felt those with her first practice session, so she knows they won't detract from her delivery. She had made it a point to write "Breathe here" in multiple places on her note cards where she tended to feel short of breathe while presenting for her friends, so she feels prepared.

"Wow, that was exhilarating! I feel like I did a pretty good job,"
Sue thinks as her teacher and peers begin to praise her speech.

Sue still has a week to go, and it has been quite a rush delivering
speeches in front of people. The experience has also been scary,
but more manageable than expected. She decides to ask various
friends here and there if she can practice in front of them. She
presents in front of a different set of friends each time, and
experiences a new set of nerves each time, but the act of public
speaking is becoming familiar to Sue.

The night before the speech is due, she gets a good night's rest.
She feels excited about the topic she will be talking about.
Although she remains a little nervous, she feels comfortable
knowing that she might just be the most prepared and confident
speaker in the room.

"This will be a little nerve-wracking, but I really put in my best
work and I think it will show," she thinks.

Speech day has finally arrived.

She sees some of her peers looking slightly nervous, yet confident
and prepared, while some other classmates are hurriedly writing
last thoughts on their note cards, and mumbling their speeches to
themselves with panicked looks on their faces.

As everyone around talks about how nervous they are, and how
they probably could have used more practice, Sue thinks, "I'm a
little bit nervous, but I definitely feel better than most of the people
here. It's kind of nice to be one of the most confident people in the
room!"

Sue delivers her speech with a smile on her face, filled with
confidence and enthusiasm.

The audience reflects her energy and leans forward in their seats as
she keeps them engaged. Some classmates even talk

enthusiastically to her after class about her topic and skilled delivery.

Sue decides she will use the rest of the semester to really hone her speaking skills and learn to truly enjoy public speaking. It may be difficult, but it's something she will have to deal with for the rest of her life, so she might as well make the most of it.

At this rate, maybe she'll get a job as some sort of speaker. It feels to Sue as if so many life and career opportunities are available to her now.

~

I don't think I need to ask, but do you see the difference?

Don't assume that these are entirely hypothetical situations. I have seen both of these scenarios play out over and over again, semester after semester with various students.

As you may have guessed, I was a lot like Sue. I was always nervous to give a speech (and I still am, to some degree). However, instead of pushing aside those uncomfortable feelings and hoping, in vain, that they would go away, I dealt with them in the best way I knew how. As a result, I came away from each public speaking course in high school and college with more confidence as a speaker.

I even became a public speaking instructor, and have continued to perform in various ways to keep my skills fresh, and to continually learn to handle nerves when I am "on stage" in a situation outside my comfort zone (Yes, I still get nervous, and so does every other performer who exists. You're not alone!).

So there you have it. The very best thing you can do to feel great about your upcoming presentation:

Prepare your material as best you can with plenty of time to practice, and practice out loud in front of people a lot.

<u>*Your Turn*</u>
Consider the following for your upcoming speech:

What mistakes have you made when preparing and/or presenting for past speeches (such as getting a late start/procrastinating, etc.)?

How can you prepare and present most effectively?

What can you do to help yourself feel more confident?

What specific action steps can you take to feel confident?

Write 5 action steps here:

1.
2.
3.
4.
5.

2. Understand and control your unique anxiety

Practice your unique way of coping with anxiety before the big day, then be prepared to have things in place to make you feel most comfortable on the day you present.

As a part of your practice sessions, before you give your final presentation, record yourself a few times to make some observations. Be sure to record yourself a few times while you're alone, but then eventually for a few people, otherwise you might trick yourself into thinking you look calm and collected, which is easy when you're presenting to no one.

How do you look in your recording? How do you sound? The good news is that when playing back your video, you might be pleasantly surprised that some of your nervousness was not actually visible.

If you tend to have a shaky voice, hands, or knees, much of the time it is not noticeable. Even if people do notice it, it's not something they are likely to fixate on. Your audience members have their own problems and fears to worry about.

And that heartbeat that sounds incredibly loud in your chest? I was always worried as a high school speaker that everyone in the classroom could hear it. The truth is that nobody can, so you can relax.

Knowing that there are no significant outward signs of your nervousness can go a long way toward helping you feel more comfortable in front of the crowd. If no one can see that you're nervous, do not draw attention to it!

I had a female student, we'll call her Joan, who was friendly, well-liked in the classroom, and a very well-spoken, passionate speaker.

Before she gave her second speech during the term, she made an announcement to let everyone know that her face would probably get extremely red during the speech, not because she was nervous, but "just because." She even went on to tell us that as a kid she would get teased and called "tomato face" because of it. However, she stated that she loved speaking with people and even giving speeches, and it was just a "weird thing" that would happen.

As I mentioned before, Joan was a great speaker, so there was no reason to get into that whole story before her presentation.

I have known many confident speakers who get a little red in the face when presenting. They are the unfortunate few who have outward signs of that adrenaline-fueled moment when they speak on stage. However, they never acknowledge it. These particular speakers are connected with the audience, and they seem to be having a good time up there! So much so, that the added color in their face is quickly forgotten.

Joan's explanation only served as a distraction to her and her audience. She ended up having a few false starts as a result, and asked if she could try her speech again at the end of the class period.

The lesson here is this: Understand how your body works, how minor (and major) nervousness affects you, and how you can best learn to appear confident and friendly on stage.

I had another student who got A's on all his assignments, and was so professional in the classroom. Yet when he had to give speeches in front of the class, he seemed flustered and his speech was choppy.

During the few minutes of feedback his peers and I offered after his speech, he said he always felt prepared for his speeches, but that his throat felt dry each time while he presented and it threw him off. I suggested that he bring a bottle of room temperature water up to the front of the room with him during his next speech, and leave it on a table that happened to be at the front of the room to the left (for those might not know, a bottle of water is perfectly acceptable in most situations when you're the presenter).

I could not believe what a difference a few sips of water had made for his next presentation. He was a completely different speaker.

Mind you, if he had realized this earlier in the semester, or talked with me about ways to combat his nerves, we could have solved the problem much earlier.

This is why you must understand your nerves and know how best to handle them. It will change everything about your presentation, from your demeanor, to the fluidity of your speech, to the way you feel while you're presenting.

Your Turn
Consider the following for your upcoming speech:

What throws you off the most when giving a speech?

What nervous habit embarrasses you the most?

What can you do to help solve these problems?

What can you do to, at the very least, not let them bother you?

Write 5 action steps here:
1.
2.
3.
4.
5.

3. Try different techniques for increasing confidence

(See the book Stage Fright *by George Griffin for a thorough list of helpful suggestions. Keep in mind, each person is nervous for different reasons, so what works for someone else might not work for you.)*

Having a bottle of water on stage while you present might not solve all your problems as a speaker, so figure out what techniques specifically work for you to eliminate your nervousness.

Eliminate Excessive Energy
You are going to have a lot of nervousness, adrenaline, and excitement pumping through you on the day of your speech, so do your best to avoid energizing yourself in other ways.

For instance, cut back on the amount of caffeine you drink that day, do some stretches, and spend some time exercising (a good run might help to calm you down). After doing these things, you will start feeling more calm and less jittery.

Relaxation
Some people spend a few minutes practicing yoga or meditation prior to a speech, or just some simple deep breathing in order to relax them.

Others find the contrast of going from such a calm state to such an adrenaline-fueled state a bit unsettling, for those people (like myself) I might suggest the following.

Power Posing
Something that's been suggested by Amy Cuddy and other body language researchers is to adopt a "high-power pose" for a few minutes in a private place prior to a high-pressure situation in order to increase your testosterone levels. Examples of this would be standing with arms and legs outstretched like an "X," or by using another pose that would physically make a person's body look bigger.

This results in feelings of power and confidence.

Humans and animals alike tend to use "power posing" when they feel powerful, but we can also power pose as a means to feel more powerful.

My students and I normally watch Cuddy's TED talk "Body Language Shapes Who You Are" at some point early in the semester, as a way to begin discussing how to handle and control potential feelings of inadequacy that are likely to crop up in a public speaking class.

My students have found the talk extremely helpful, and many of them have even told me they practice high-power posing (basically, standing like Wonder Woman for two minutes in a private place) before job interviews and speeches to appear more confident, and also to *feel* more confident.

Fake It 'til You Make It
Over the years I have used a mix of different things to help relax my own nerves.

One of the major ones is to act confident, and internally tell yourself that you feel confident, prepared, and excited to be on stage. I have heard other people say they just accept that they are a ball of nerves, but I choose the "fake it 'til you make it" approach (another gem of wisdom from Amy Cuddy).

I essentially get into character.

I make sure I'm not checking email on my phone, or hunched over in some way that makes me appear small before a presentation (this is called "low-power posing," which can actually make a person more nervous due to an increase in cortisol levels).

I also make it a point to talk to people in the crowd before I perform, whether it is for a musical performance or a lecture. It establishes a friendly and enthusiastic environment for you and the audience, which decreases some of the uncomfortable feelings of uncertainty or discomfort before a presentation.

Positive Self-talk
Positive self-talk is another technique my students have credited with helping them feel more confident as speakers. So if you have a habit of sabotaging your presentations, or internally doubting your skills, change that inner monologue to something constructive.

Be your own biggest cheerleader!

I will end this section with a recent post of mine on the website happyprofessor.com that was inspired by every public speaking book I have read that at some point discussed the importance of positive self-talk and positive thinking.

It doesn't matter what type of situation you find yourself in, whether it's a speech, job interview, play, a long project that you are nervous about completing successfully, or any of the other multitude of things that have the potential to put someone ill at ease.

Harness the power of positivity.

~

Let Your Mind Wander, and Find Yourself on a True Journey
May 11, 2015 post on happyprofessor.com by Erin Lovell Ebanks

Positive thinking is a powerful thing.

It is the best way to get from where you are to where you would like to be, in school, work, relationships, and life.

Most people are not as familiar as they should be with the power of positive thinking; they tend to be more familiar with the nagging voice in their head (that sounds a lot like them). It tells them they're making bad decisions, they should be ashamed of themselves, and that they will never amount to anything.

That voice can be pretty brutal.

But what if we changed this?

Somehow, right around the time I left for college as an 18-year-old, I turned off that voice (for the most part). I decided to start cheering for myself instead, applauding my efforts, even when they failed. If the "mean" voice managed to make an appearance, the "nice" voice would shoo her away.

One of the best tips I can give my college students to help them present a successful speech, is to imagine (repeatedly) that they have already given a successful speech.

They shouldn't just think to themselves, "You'll do great, you'll do great, etc.." That's a good start, but you should try to actually feel it, live it, try your best to mentally practice the situation before it happens, and be specific.

If you were giving a speech, this might be part of the positive visualization you would use (you can fill in the blanks as you let your mind get creative):

Imagine yourself standing at the front of the room (How do you feel? Happy? Confident? Remember, nothing negative!).

You feel that you are dressed perfectly for the occasion (What exactly are you wearing? Jewelry? A tie? What color is your shirt? It looks great!) as you look out at the audience (31 people to be exact, they all look supportive, and they are smiling, eager to hear your message).

You start your speech and it is already a success (you sound enthusiastic as a speaker, you feel confident, and the audience leans in showing their interest).

Doesn't that feel great?

It's no wonder professional athletes who practice positive visualization in place of physical practice do just as well when the big game comes around. It's no wonder that so many successful people spend a significant amount of time imagining positive outcomes and even take the time to visually represent those outcomes on vision boards.

I recently listened to a book on tape, and could not believe that- yet again- I was hearing about visualization.

It was the book *High Impact Communication: How to Build Charisma, Credibility, and Trust* by Bert Decker, and yet again, another communication expert was discussing the importance of positive thinking and visualization.

As the story goes, the author's wife had her own writing aspirations, and he recalls her spending as much time writing her first book as she did imagining what outfit she would wear to a jam-packed book signing for her hit novel (these were all hopes and dreams; she had no previous success as an author).

Sure enough, both the writing and the fantasizing paid off, and played out exactly as this new author had hoped.

You don't have to be a professional athlete, successful author, public speaker, or wealthy entrepreneur to practice visualization and picture life unfolding the way you would like it to.

Start small.

I pictured myself teaching enthusiastic college students ("enthusiastic" being the key word here), feeling successful regardless of what my income might be, and being happy with the simple things life has to offer.

I didn't always visualize intentionally, but you know those moments that you find yourself tuned out during a conversation, or lost in thought while you lay in bed at night? That's when the magic (science, actually) happened for me.

The trick is to train your kind, positive voice to make an appearance more often. That voice has big plans for you, and will support all the ideas you have in the making.

Be kind to yourself, then let your mind wander, and find yourself on a true journey.

Your Turn
Consider the following for your upcoming speech:

What positive things can you tell yourself when you are nervous about an upcoming speech?

How can you tune out your self-doubt and negative thoughts?

What positive details can you specifically visualize about your speech?

Positive visualization exercise:

Write out what your experience with your next speech will be in one long paragraph, with as many positive specifics and feelings as you can. Write it out in detail as if it is happening to you right now, you are speaking for your actual audience, in the room you will be presenting in, you are doing an incredible job, and the audience just loves you. Use my example in the blog post above to help guide you.

After you have finished writing, write another paragraph describing how the above activity made you feel. Do you feel more confident? Excited?

Do this positive visualization exercise 5 more times before your next speech. You can write it out, read what you wrote here the initial time, or play it over in your head from memory.

4. Frame your anxiety differently

Lastly here, I want you to change the way you view your performance anxiety. Do you see it as the enemy or as your partner?

Another TED talk I show my students (typically just before final exam week, for obvious reasons) is Kelly McGonigal's "How to Make Stress Your Friend."

McGonigal is a health psychologist, who claims that if you view stress as something that happens in order to help you meet a challenge, the stress will have a healthier effect on you. If you view it as an annoyance with the potential to harm you, it may instead be bad for your health. (Watch it yourself to improve your life and perspective!)

Personally, I like to think that anxiety, or whatever you might want to call it, is actually helping my body accomplish what I have set out to do. Over the years, I have started noticing what a different path that mindset has taken me down.

Have you ever noticed that when someone is not nervous about a performance and/or just doesn't really care, regardless of how much they have prepared the content, it falls flat?

I was lecturing for a summer class a few years back, and I had become a bit too comfortable, and maybe a bit complacent in the classroom, especially over the summer term with just a handful of students present.

That particular day, I didn't feel that adrenaline rush that I was used to it.

The result? A truly awful lecture.

I failed to come up with the examples I was reaching for, and to make the connections I wanted to between ideas. That adrenaline was nowhere to be found to help me put the pieces back together.

I struggled through the entire 20 minutes.

I had done that particular lecture many times before, and I have presented it many times since, but that experience sticks vividly in my mind.

It serves as a reminder that we all need some of that heart-pounding excitement that surrounds a performance, because it makes the outcome better. As a side note, do keep in mind that there is such a thing as too much anxiety, and too little anxiety. Try your best to figure out how to maintain the best level for you, using some of the suggestions in the previous section.

Lastly, I would like to explain the way our perspective of stress can really change certain outcomes in our life, as I have seen it play out in my own life and in others.

I have a very good friend whose life is not all that different from mine. I would assume we are both equal parts introvert and extrovert, and feel the same amount of stress about an upcoming presentation.

However, from the time we were teens, instead of seeing a speaking opportunity as a chance to grow as a person, she would hold some resentment and sore feelings toward the person who had put her in the speaking situation. In general, this very capable (but frustrated) friend would harbor negative feelings about the whole situation and upcoming speech.

Our objective experiences were similar, but she saw the speech as punishment from someone who did not have her best interests at heart, while I saw speaking opportunities as an enormous compliment and vote of confidence from someone who I assumed thought very highly of me!

To this day, these perspectives for the two of us have remained about the same over the past decade. Although, after being asked to give several speeches for her company, this friend of mine (a fantastic speaker by the way) is eventually starting to come around and change her perspective due to the praise she had received about her speaking skills from her superiors.

She still believes the stress is damaging her health, but small steps toward a different viewpoint are better than nothing. On the other hand, I tend to prefer a little bit of perpetual stress in my life (Though I'll admit for the students out there- I may not have been the biggest fan during my college years!).

For me these days, feeling a little bit of tension about upcoming projects means that I am challenging myself as a person and growing on a daily basis.

What's not to be happy about?

Try your hand at changing the way you view new experiences and performance opportunities.

Yes, it's scary and stressful sometimes, and it will take practice to continually see the positives associated with uncomfortable situations that might arise, but I promise you it is a worthy goal to pursue.

Your Turn
Consider the following for your upcoming speech:

How can you change your perspective of your nervousness?

How has that adrenaline rush helped you when you have had to present/perform?

In what ways can you decrease that adrenaline rush to the level at which it can help you the most?

~

If at this point you're thinking, "Wait. I still have to put in the work? And my nerves aren't even going to completely go away? I thought this section was supposed to inject me with permanent confidence! I thought you had a magic solution for me!"

I'll try my best to talk you off the ledge.

The nerves will never go away.

Let me say that again:

The nerves will never go away.

I know it's hard to hear.

The same way that you simply cannot wake up after one year of a sedentary lifestyle and decide to run a marathon that morning, you cannot wake up one day and say "I'm not going to be nervous for this speech at all. How cool!"

However, just like one might train for a marathon, and be proud that they were able to finish it, you will be able to train for your speech and feel accomplished afterward. The more you practice speaking and the more you run, the more successful the outcome will be and the easier it will get.

However, your muscles will always get fatigued and you will always feel nervous; that's just human biology, though you will get used to managing that.

There are some professional speakers who claim to love speaking and never feel real nervousness (Are you as jealous as I am?).

However, other speakers who are just as successful claim that they still get nervous each and every time (Are you as relieved as I am?).

These speakers have developed great ways to cope with it, and they will never let it hold them back, but it will also never go away. It might be nice if it did, but without the challenge, I don't know that people would work so hard to get better at it.

Again, if you don't get nervous when you present for a crowd, I have no idea what your public speaking experiences feel like for you, but enjoy your superpower!

If you get nervous every time, here are some things that might help:

- Pick a topic you are already familiar with.
- Take your preparation and practice to the extreme, like I have mentioned in some examples and my personal examples in the previous sections.
- Practice in front of people time and time again, over and over, leading up to the day of the presentation.
- Join a club that will require you to give speeches. Toastmasters is a great one to join. Each week you have the opportunity to speak. I can promise after a year of doing this, you will feel a huge difference in your confidence level. You might also make some new friends.
- Do one thing every day that makes you nervous. Whether it's staying to talk to an intimidating teacher after class (for whatever reason you can come up with), striking up a conversation with a stranger in a coffee shop, or doing some street performing, stretching yourself like this on a daily basis will do wonders for your confidence. I know this last one might sound a bit extreme, but Google some examples and see what you can come up with. Taking an instrument of your choice to a popular area in your town might just change your life. You will definitely get used to people staring at you, and might also make some extra money!

Your Turn
Pick two clubs/organizations you can join to start giving presentations on a regular basis.

1.
2.

If you're willing to try some more daring approaches, like joining Toastmasters or street performing, write it below. Include how you think it might be beneficial to you.

_____

_____

_____

Step 3
<u>Have Fun</u>

Do you know how lucky you are?

Do you know how much fun this can be?

You've been given the opportunity to share your unique message, perspective, and voice with an audience.

Now stop thinking about everything you're feeling for a minute.

What about them? The people who came to watch you speak. Don't they deserve to see the real you? Don't they deserve the chance to hear a worthwhile message?

Be kind to them, entertain them, let them have fun, and make their day that much better. This type of attitude can make everything about your own experience that much better, too.

Here are some important things we will touch on during Step 3:
1. Get into the right frame of mind
2. Enjoy showcasing your unique personality and message
3. Leverage your skills to gain value and further advance your career
4. Embrace these experiences for personal fulfillment

I have a few personal stories about audience satisfaction and personal fulfillment that I hope will change the way you look at performing.

When I get up to lecture for my students, occasionally I might think:

"I really don't feel like doing this today. If I lecture in four classes this morning, I will be on my feet all day, my voice is going to get tired, and I'll be exhausted by the time I get home."

Or I might start worrying about the way I come off, or the way I phrase something.

Either way. How selfish am I!

Positive thoughts about yourself are great, but indulging in negativity is just selfish and disrespectful of your audience. I do realize I am throwing myself under the bus here, but we all do this at some time or another. The key is to realize your self-destructive thoughts and make appropriate changes.

You are allowed to worry a little bit about yourself before you give a speech because, understandably, you want your audience to get the best version of you possible.

However, once you are on stage, it's about them and positive energy.

When I'm at my best, I'll think to myself, "My students don't look that excited today. They know it's lecture day. Little do they know we're going to incorporate a bunch of TV and YouTube clips to relate to the textbook material. I am so excited to see their change in demeanor by the end of the hour. They are going to have so much fun! "

And they do.

We laugh together, I ask them what each video clip has to do with informative speaking, miscommunication, vocal tone, or other textbook concepts, and they participate and give their input.

I can barely control my giddiness at seeing how much fun they are having, how much they are learning and listening (even when it's me talking instead of YouTube), and how much they did *not* expect a lecture class period to turn out this way. They leave the room with smiles on their faces, lingering laughter, happy shouts of, "See you next class, Mrs. Ebanks!" as completely different people than when they walked into class.

I am not perfect up there during my lectures, but I'm real, I know my material, and I know how to connect with the audience in a way that will ensure they leave an hour later having added value to their life in some way.

That is the goal for every speaker. Add value to the lives of your audience members, especially if you are a teacher or paid speaker.

~

I have another story to share about not being too concerned with yourself, and learning to let it go.

On occasion, I perform at open mic nights. Unlike my experience speaking in the classroom to my students literally hundreds of times over the years (that's some quality practice!), I've only performed on stage at open mic nights about 15 times in recent years.

It takes a lot of time for me to prepare for a musical performance, but I do it because it is a worthwhile experience and something I ultimately enjoy. In my preparation, I learn how to play a set of 3 new songs on the guitar for my performances, memorize the lyrics of those new songs (and I am truly awful at learning song lyrics), put my own spin on things, and then practice a few dozen times by myself (sitting or standing, whichever the venue calls for).

After which, I practice for various groups of friends to see how the nerves affect my performance, and if I might have a hard time catching my breath in some spots (it is amazing how difficult and unnatural breathing becomes once you are in front of a crowd).

I also visit the venue at least once during a previous open mic night to see how they run things, what type of songs are played, how many songs each performer plays, which of my guitars would be most appropriate to bring, and what the audience is like (Remember audience analysis? It's important when it comes to most things in life, not just speaking.)

I probably put in at least a good 20 to 30 hours of practice before I get up on stage, just as you would do throughout your preparation, research, and speech practices before the big day.

The amazing thing is my final performance is usually much better than all the practice sessions (and yes, I record and watch each rehearsal and final "show" like I have recommended to you).

I attribute a good performance to the extensive preparation I have done, leading up to the event.

Now here is why it's important to "fake it 'til you make it."

I experienced something that was new for me the last time I set my mind on singing and playing my guitar for a crowd.

I didn't try to 'fake it' at all the last time I performed at an open mic night. It had been two years since I had performed somewhat regularly, and I didn't have much time to put into this hobby anymore (not to worry, it is only because I do so many other fun things that have been taking up my time- like speaking for a living).

Needless to say, I wanted to go out with a bang, at least for the time being.

There were a few problems with that, though.

Problem number one was that "going out with a bang" is way too much pressure for one person. Problem two was that I only had the time to practice for two small groups of people ahead of time (which just does not cut it for me). Problem three was that I barely ate anything all day, and it was the most nervous I can remember feeling for any performance.

This was the outcome:
- I was petrified

- My mouth was incredibly dry because I had barely had anything to eat or drink (which is not ideal for singing 3 songs), which had also made me a little weak
- I forgot to fake my confidence

I was so disappointed afterward. This was me going out with a bang?

I watched the playback of the video afterward, assuming that every word I almost forgot while I was singing, and every chord that I almost did not hit, had made me completely blow it.

The silver lining? I actually sounded great.

I was so confused. I watched the video again. I thought I was missing something. Was this the same performance that happened just a few minutes ago?

The only giveaway that I was not having a good time in the video was that I didn't smile. Not once. I didn't look like a deer in the headlights like I thought I had, but I looked angry (probably because I had been frustrated with myself that I was "blowing it" up there).

How could I have been so wrong?

This is why I tell my students to record their speeches in class and watch them later.

Most of the time they balk at that suggestion, saying they would be too nervous to watch it afterward. But it would be so valuable if they did.

Most of the time, those little slip ups that happen during your presentation are not noticeable to your audience. In fact, your speech probably turned out much better than you thought it did. I have students who never quite get over the fact that they "messed up" their speech, despite how many times I try to convince them they did much better than they imagined.

Consider the confidence you could gain from just letting yourself be impressed by you!

Luckily, I had recorded my open mic night performance and was pleasantly surprised. I just needed to lighten up and smile next time. So I did.

I had already planned to do another open mic night the very next day, since I knew I would already be prepared and accustomed to playing in front of a crowd. I know myself, and after an initial performance, I am usually much more comfortable during a repeat performance.

I felt great. I learned my lesson the night before. I told my friends in the crowd to use their nonverbals to remind me to smile during the performance, in case I forgot, and I made it a point to enjoy those 10 to 15 minutes.

Who knew when I would be able to invest the time, energy, and adrenaline needed to experience a moment like this again? I promised myself it would be positive, valuable, and memorable for me and the audience.

And it was.

The audience enjoyed some of my original music and talked to me about it afterward. I smiled while I was singing on stage, and I really had a good time. During the set I kept thinking, "This is great. I'm really having fun. What a relief. If I could do this every day, and becoming acclimated to the musician's lifestyle, like I feel I am right now, it would be so much fun. What a cool life."

Alas, I already spend the majority of my free time teaching and writing, which are also some great loves of my life, so nothing is lost.

But you, my friend.

You are going to be performing a lot in your life. What the situation might be is irrelevant. If you have picked up this book, it is because you're going beyond the basics of surviving an introductory speech course or presenting a one-time business presentation.

Somewhere in the back of your mind, you know an audience will perpetually be in your future, and you are preparing yourself now.

Becoming skilled at speaking is well worth the investment, and this book will be a huge help on your journey.

You are going to need a lot of practice (see my tips from Step 2), and a lot of repetition, and you will need to figure out exactly how you operate as a performer.

Reading this book is the perfect step to opening new doors, more opportunities, money, fulfillment, and a lot of fun.

1. Get into the right frame of mind

Don't just try to survive, do everything you can to make presenting a moment that can change your life.

I understand if you are a college student, or someone in a temporary job, that you might not be thinking about how your day to day routine at this very moment will impact the next 20 years of your life, but I hope I can have some influence here in helping you think ahead.

This can be a life-changing experience for you.

Here are a few steps to make that happen:

- Take it seriously

Do what you can to make your presentation an experience like my eventual lecture and open mic night experiences were in the stories above. This is where the magic is.

If you can get that positivity flowing right before, during, and right after your performance, you are experiencing something much different than what most new speakers experience. You have crossed the threshold into a valuable territory.

What can you do with this skill you are building, now that you're not scared? How can you keep practicing to maintain those skills (again, see my tips in Step 2)?

- Gain something tangible

Make your speech valuable, and record it for future job opportunities and projects that might come your way.

Speaking is a valuable skill to have. If your first presentation is not as great as you would like it to be, record every single one until you have at least a few one-minute-long clips that you can put on a professional website or YouTube to impress a future employer or contact.

- Be a positive influence

Make a positive difference in the lives of your audience members.

Since you have already learned how to have the confidence you need, channel it to enjoy this time with the people listening to you. Share something of value that you can enjoy, that the audience can enjoy, and that will make a difference.

Teach them something valuable that they might not have otherwise learned. I have a number of students who choose to give speeches about reducing stress, practicing yoga, or getting more sleep for better health. I truly believe the speakers enjoy sharing their topics to improve the lives of their classmates, and I believe the audience gains improved knowledge and potentially better health as a result.

Give your audience the value of a meaningful message you have the power to share.

- Don't take it *too* seriously

I realize I am contradicting the first bullet point listed here, but loosen up!

A few pieces of (somewhat unconventional) advice that have always stuck with me are:

1. Nobody will be over-analyzing your speech as much as you, not even a teacher or boss.
2. Everyone has messed up a performance, even the greats. If you don't believe me, read *Stage Fright: 40 Stars Tell You How They Beat America's #1 Fear* by Berry and Edelstein.
3. Worrying never solves anything. It is a complete waste of effort.
4. In a hundred years, will anyone really care?

Your Turn
Consider the following for your upcoming speech:

How can you gain value from your next speech?

How can you present it, and present yourself, in a way that will leave you with something tangible that might impress a future employer?

How can you make the audience's day during your next presentation?

2. Enjoy showcasing your unique personality and message

Another piece of advice that I try to live by:

"Don't leave a situation feeling like you didn't let people know who you really were, and what you have to offer."

I can certainly tell you that I felt I had failed at that after I "bombed" the open mic night, but I lived up to the piece of advice above during round two. So I was able to be proud of myself for really showing people who I was and what I was capable of doing.

Here's how to get the most positivity from your experience:

- Smile and laugh

Don't be so serious. Endear yourself to the audience. Smile and laugh with them, and like I mentioned above, show them that you are there to make their day a little better.

If you tell the audience you're scared or are not a big fan of public speaking (many people do this hoping it will earn them sympathy from the audience), it only makes the crowd uncomfortable, and makes the experience unpleasant.

- Share

Share knowledge and personal (appropriate) stories with the audience. Share a moment and establish a meaningful connection.

Your speech does not have to be all business. If you take note of some of the more meaningful and captivating speeches you have listened to in your lifetime, they did not consist primarily of statistics and source citations. They had heart.

- Audience participation

You can even have the audience share their own stories as well.

Get some audience participation. Depending on how long your presentation is, you may want to limit audience involvement to a few "yes or no" questions scattered throughout the speech to keep them interested. If you plan on presenting for an hour or so, you can ask some open-ended questions and really develop a relationship with the group.

- Activities

Again, if your presentation will be at least one hour long, you might want to incorporate some purposeful activities into the presentation to make the experience more fun and dynamic for everyone involved.

For example, if you plan on teaching some of the material in this book to a group of people during an hour-long session, you probably don't want everyone to sit quietly and read it to themselves to learn in the most effective and engaging way. You will want to incorporate some discussions, personal experiences, video clips, and other activities.

In the Resources section of this book, I have included some specific activities that speech teachers or speech workshop facilitators can use to accompany the material their students might read in this book. It wakes up the audience, makes them more interested, and is a way to make the material memorable and relatable.

- Discuss

In a short presentation, you will most likely be the only one "discussing" a topic.

That is essentially what an extemporaneous speech is, a one-sided conversation in which the audience feels you are the expert. In a long presentation, however, you can get the whole group to weigh in on some topics.

A friend of mine was recently asked to speak at a marriage retreat in front of an audience of 20 couples. After opening her speech with some minor audience participation (a quiz testing how much they know about marriage), they ended up having a discussion about each of the questions. She had not exactly planned for that, but she said it was a "hoot," and much more fun than if she had "talked at" them the entire time.

Of course, it depends on what the rules and requirements are for the event, how much/if you are being paid to follow a certain structure, and how much flexibility and time you have, but this is another form of a perfectly acceptable presentation.

- Learn

The reason some people move forward to make presenting an integral part of their life is because they are gaining something. Each time you deliver a speech, you will learn about your topic, your audience, and yourself.

You will grow in a number of ways each time you're on stage, and that is one of the most rewarding gifts a person can ask for.

Your Turn
Consider the following for your upcoming speech:

How can you be engaging, professional, and have fun with your audience at the same time while presenting?

In what way would it be appropriate to get your audience involved during your presentation?

What do you plan on learning during the preparation process?

What do you plan on learning during the presentation process?

What do you want the audience to get out of your next speech?

Remember to have fun with them, and don't forget to smile!

3. Leverage your skills to gain value and further advance your career

Again, public speaking is one of the most valuable and thrilling things you can experience in your life.

Just as I shared in my previous stories and examples about being *extremely* prepared, understand that you can practice enough so that you don't just "kind of" overcome the fear, but so that you can start to enjoy yourself, observe what happens while you perform, and benefit from the positive audience response.

Take this time to realize you can leverage these new skills to make yourself a standout in school clubs, your career, or even the public speaking circuit. The ability to speak in public will give you such a competitive advantage in life. It is a great way to find a fulfilling job, start your own company, be a leader, give speeches for a living, or simply grow as a person.

One of the best ways to use public speaking to your advantage these days is to record your professional presentations, and keep them on a professional website for future employers (if they are appropriate and impressive, that is).

It didn't occur to me until more recently that I should have some sort of professional social media presence. As I mentioned previously, I noticed one of my grad school friends and fellow TAs was always recording her lectures and going a little above and beyond with extracurricular activities and performance opportunities. I thought she was just a little obsessed with herself.

I didn't realize that she was actually brilliant.

She owned a domain name that displayed her full name, and on that site she kept a sort of digital resume. She worked for a theater company, wrote plays, did small TV hosting gigs, and had bigger plans that involved getting a second Master's degree in Theater and more acting jobs. Since she had to put in the work anyway, why not make it the best it could be, and use it to promote herself for other job opportunities.

Have you done that?

I have now, and even though I feel I got a late start, it paid off in ways I couldn't have imagined: financially, job opportunity-wise, and it helped me to almost effortlessly build an extensive list of valuable social contacts.

I can promise you life is not all about making more money.

However, if you can enjoy speaking in public, you have an edge over other people in your field, and it makes you more valuable as an employee or business owner. It is one of the most fun and easy ways to achieve this.

You may not realize it at the moment, but every one of those things will be essential in propelling yourself forward with exciting new projects that will be of benefit to you as a person.

If you do not own a professional domain name already, look for URLs with your first and last name that are available, and buy the one that suits you best (it's affordable, and well worth the investment).

Start building a resume there. If you're not ready for it to be available to the world yet, just don't tell anyone about it. There is so much content out there in cyberspace, no one will accidentally stumble upon your site unless you are already making a name for yourself and people are actively looking you up.

It doesn't matter if you are starting off slow with a small amount of content. Make it a goal to collect impressive accomplishments for this online resume within just the next year, and you will make some significant progress.

I have a short story here.

A friend of mine worked as a Student Life Coordinator at a local community college, and she eventually wrote a book about it. She could have easily done what many other people who have written a book do: sit back and wait for it to sell itself.

Instead, she leveraged her love of communicating, as well as her personality, confidence, and skills in public speaking to turn her book into a well-paying, fulfilling, and successful career, where she got to be the boss.

She started speaking to hundreds of students and faculty at various colleges. She started slow and locally, but kept building her website, YouTube channel, and social media presence. Eventually, other schools were noticing her impressive keynote speeches online, and contacting her to present to their schools.

This meant free flights, hotels, and a nice paycheck for going on a trip and speaking to people. This is part of what I'm getting at when I say public speaking is a valuable skill to have.

When she wasn't traveling, she worked from home on building her social networks, improving her speaking skills, and developing new speeches that would speak more specifically to certain audiences.

She didn't stop there.

When she was traveling, she would network with the people she met, make plans to meet up for dinner, coffee, and whatever else she could during her short stays.

The contacts she made and the people she spent an hour with here and there on trips have now led her to even more valuable contacts. These are people who are now helping her to conduct research for her second book, and to launch her company into something bigger. Would you have gone the extra step to make your product a success through public speaking?

Think about it. It is so easy to come up with excuses, and rationalize with reasons not to get up there on stage.

Maybe you can think of other ways you could be successful launching your product. However, personal and public communication will be one of the most effective routes every time, and I think you know that, too.

I hope by now you understand that public speaking is not just the most effective way to succeed, but also the most fun.

Here are a few things you should do now that you have come out of your shell and embraced the joy of public speaking:

- Apply for well-paying jobs that require some public speaking. Many people are intimidated by these positions, but they are normally much more fun than the usual 9 to 5 desk job.
- Go to networking events and make important contacts to help you in school and/or in your career.

Your Turn
Consider the following for your upcoming speech:

How you get value from your next speech?

How can you take this presentation one step further (i.e. post a clip of your presentation on your personal website, decide to do your senior thesis on your speech topic, research and present your speech in a way that will help you get an interview with a company you want to be hired by)?

I challenge you to record your speech. If it's not perfect, find a 30 second clip that looks impressive. If there is nothing professional or impressive about it (and that might just be you being hard on yourself!), no worries, just try again for your next presentation.

4. Embrace these experiences for personal fulfillment

It's not all about getting ahead.

I don't want you to think speaking and networking are all about working your way up to the most impressive job and the best salary.

Ask any college professor, and they will tell you it is not about the money, and it never will be. We have lectures, discussions, and pep talks with our classes because it is incredibly fulfilling to help *them* gain something of value.

We get to share the content we care about with people who, if we do our job correctly, will care about it, too. We have the privilege of helping people learn, grow, and feel good about their progress.

As a high school student, I never participated in class discussions or raised my hand to give an answer. My worst nightmare was being called on to contribute because I was scared to speak out.

Every time I had a really good answer, and wanted to proudly share it with class, no matter how badly I wanted to say it, the fear always won. Inevitably, I would hear someone else give the answer, and I would envy the credit they got, and be disappointed in myself.

This happened almost on a daily basis, but eventually I was just so tired of being scared, that I started to speak out in big ways, like taking on leadership roles, and eventually becoming a public speaking instructor.

It was like a huge burden had been lifted.

I have never felt more fulfilled in my entire life than when I stopped letting fear run the show, and I have never stopped speaking up.

This is what all public speaking boils down to. The feeling of accomplishment and self-satisfaction you get once you have overcome one of the biggest invisible obstacles most people will ever face. That feeling is incomparable.

So start taking chances, gain the confidence you deserve, and have fun.

Your Turn
How can you take a chance with public speaking in terms of networking or applying for an internship/job you have been intrigued yet intimidated by (How introverted or extroverted you are will be a factor. A big step for one person might be a very small step to someone else, so be sure to challenge yourself, specifically.)?

In what ways do you think public speaking might play a role in your life's accomplishments, now or later in life?

I challenge you to join a club or organization that will occasionally ask you to speak publicly. It might be scary at first, but give it a year (yes, a year), and you will be amazed at what you have gained.

~

If you have had some awkward public speaking moments in your past, and you find yourself allowing it to hold you back, this small addition is for you.

Don't let it stop you forever. We have all survived and lived to tell about it.

In honor of making light of public speaking, and showing that even those in the speaking field have had their share of mishaps, I present you with some embarrassing speaking moments:

Embarrassing Public Speaking Moments

"I was two minutes into my door-to-door sales pitch before I realized I wasn't talking to the homeowner, but the owner's 13-year-old daughter. It was an extremely awkward moment, and I still laugh about it from time to time."

~Financial Analyst at Lockheed Martin, former sales rep for Comcast

"I actually interviewed for the wrong job once. It would have been really funny if they offered the position to me, but that didn't happen. I was just a little bit humiliated for a while."

~Marketing Analytics rep for Uber

"As a new TA, I walked into class on the first day and started taking roll. I even told the students that they might be in the wrong room when I noticed there were so many absences! I didn't realize I was the one in the wrong room until the actual teacher walked in. I certainly heard some giggles as I walked out."

~Psychology professor, MA, and speaker

"My senior year of college in my last class ever, I had to give an oral presentation, and realized after the fact that my fly was down. Not the worst thing ever, but definitely unfortunate."

~Communication professor

"On my way out the door for work one day, during the days when my kids were still little, I noticed I had somehow cut myself on the middle of my back. I was in a rush, and the only bandages in the house were Muppet Baby themed (that's life with two little girls), so that was what I used. I quickly put one on, made sure I looked professional, and headed to the office. I had to present during a meeting that morning, and little did I know the colorful bandage (with all the Muppet Babies present) was very noticeable whenever I leaned over, turning my back to the crowd, to adjust the computer settings for our presentation. It wasn't until the end of the day that someone pointed it out to me. It's become a funny story my kids

bring up once in a while."
~CEO of a computer software company

"At one point during my presentation at an annual faculty meeting, I approached the audio visuals and squatted down to adjust the equipment. At that very moment an audible tearing sound filled the entire room. Everyone was speechless as my pants tore from the waist right down the middle. I was horrified! In any case, my marvelous assistant reacted on the spot and brought me her sweater to tie around my waist. I never acknowledged or brought additional attention to what occurred, but instead continued speaking, remained professional, and continued with my performance."
~ Director of the School of Professional and Career Education for a private university

"I'm sure there are more than I can remember. One just happened last month, when I was making the toast to our graduating college seniors, and I used incorrect English. It was in front of the students, my staff, my president, and faculty. I handled it by acknowledging it and moving on, but unfortunately the speech is on the University's YouTube channel with hundreds of views. You just have to understand that mistakes and embarrassment are going to happen. It's par for the course, it's part of my job, and I'm not perfect, but I'll keep moving forward!"
~Executive Director of Alumni Engagement for a private

university

"I was making a final presentation to the senior leadership team of a university I was consulting with, and I was delivering my final report. We were using a large screen to speak with others being Skyped in. Right in the middle of my presentation, a message popped up on the large screen we were using to talk with team members from afar; it was a Skype text from my brother, and included unprofessional language. The president started cracking up, as well as the entire room, and then when I saw it, I tried to quickly scramble to close it out! So lesson learned. Be sure to warn those family members you occasionally communicate with via Skype, that you are going to be using the program at a specific time, for professional reasons and in a public way, so don't message me."

~Executive Director of Alumni Engagement for a private university

"Probably one of my more embarrassing moments as a communicator was preaching to a room full of high school students. I was on an elevated platform, maybe about 4-feet off the ground, so I was looking over the front row and into the middle of the audience. There was a couple that was making out in the front row the whole time I was preaching, and I was the only one in the room that didn't know it. Everyone was completely distracted and I had no idea."

~Student Ministry Director

I thought I'd finish off with my own, long drawn out tale of shame:

"I have a couple embarrassing moments. When I was in high school, I did a demonstration speech to walk the class through the steps of carving a pumpkin. While I was using my little carving tools to carve a circle around the top to begin the process, I was so nervous that I pulled the pumpkin stem right off, so I couldn't grab anything to actually get access into the pumpkin to continue the steps of my speech. I was completely taken off guard, stopped dead in my tracks, and stared at my teacher for a significant amount of time. I have no idea what happened after that- I completely blocked it out, but my instinct (or pride) tells me that I somehow managed to get through it and do a decent job, because I did get an A in that class! As for my other story, a few years back, I completely bombed a lecture. I recall feeling a little tired and complacent that day, and I just struggled to make sense for a good 20 minutes. It was a very good lesson (for me), though. You can be sure that never happened again!"

~ Erin, MA, Communication instructor, author, and survivor of speeches gone wrong

~

I hope you see how much fun public speaking can be, regardless of whether you experience embarrassing moments or not.

We have all been there, and we will all mess up again.

Your experiences do not have to be perfect. Just remember to always prepare, build your confidence, and work toward making public speaking a fun skill that you can be proud of. It can be one of the most rewarding and fulfilling parts of your life.

Here's to a brand new you.

Interviews with Public Speakers

This section is comprised of various interviews with different people who speak publicly as part of their career (whether they intended for it to happen or not!).

I was incredibly inspired by some of the responses I got. I have a feeling this might end up being your favorite section in the book.

I had the honor of getting candid feedback from those in the media, professional consulting, ministry, business, and higher education.

Take some tips from the people you are about to meet here.

Their journey from new speaker to professional speaker took a lot of hard work, time, and courage, so don't lose patience with yourself if you're not a pro yet (it'll take a few reads of this book and some years of practice!).

I *know* you have what it takes to be just as successful, just like the individuals you are about to meet.

Speakers in Media

<u>Writer and Author</u>

Other side projects/jobs that include presenting/performing:

Speaking on behalf of my books, and hosting a TV show

How long have you been presenting/performing as part of your job?

3 years

How often do you have to present in front of a crowd?

Once a month

How big are the audiences you present in front of?

100-1,000 people

How did you feel as a high school or college student giving speeches in class? Describe what went through your head and what you felt when you were assigned a speech, once you were preparing, the day of the speech, and once you were speaking.

When assigned a speech I always felt a little nervous, but also excited. I enjoy presenting. While preparing I'd always start by thinking of my audience- what would they find most entertaining? How can I make this a part of a class they enjoy versus being bored to death? I always got excited by the challenge of having a part in trying to make a class engaging, even if only for 5-10 minutes.

The day of, I always woke up a little excited, but I also felt so physically nervous. I never dreaded speeches, but I always felt the physical rush of "OMG I'M ABOUT TO GET IN FRONT OF PEOPLE, HOPEFULLY THEY DON'T KICK ME OUT OF THE TRIBE!!" You know, that primal crazy stuff we feel before getting up in front of people, as if we literally might die. That never goes away completely, but I've found ways to just sit with it, let it do this thing, and breathe. I know that it's really going to be okay, and that since I did my part (e.g. practicing, preparing) that it could even be a chance to do something really good.

How do you feel now as someone who gives speeches for a living or as part of your job? Describe what goes through your head and what do you feel like when you get a speaking gig, once you're preparing, the day of the speech, and once you start speaking.

It's very similar to the first questions, since presenting was always something I enjoyed. However, the biggest difference as a professional is that in some ways I get more nervous; it actually matters more to me than it did in school. And the stakes just feel higher because someone isn't just "grading" me, they're paying me! And that makes me feel like I really need to do a good job. So it's more of an intense experience than it was in school, but also more gratifying when it's over.

How did you make progress from the time you were a student to now? What did you do to improve as a speaker?

I watched lots of great speeches and presentations, I read books on speaking, and I took LOTS of notes as I watched speakers (and great teachers) over the years on what they did really well. I also took mental notes of what bored me in classrooms and in speeches and tried to get a good handle on what I found engaging and what I didn't. Then I tried to implement those things when I was planning a speech. A lot of it was just trial and error, speaking all the time and making mental notes of what went well and what I could do better each and every time, always based on what I thought the audience got out of it.

What did you do to increase your confidence?

I kept speaking over and over again. You'll be amazed at how people will come up to you afterward and tell you how much they liked your speech. As long as you are being your authentic self (e.g. not stiffly reading a speech that isn't really you), trust me, people will want to talk to you afterward. We love when people share themselves with us publicly, because deep down we know it's a brave thing to do, we know it's scary, and we just love those who are brave enough to do it for us. Because we need each other's stories.

What do you do to stay in the moment and enjoy your time presenting in front of a crowd?

I try to look in a few people's eyes and say a few sentences of the speech before moving on to another person, as if it's just them and me having a conversation.

What positive thoughts go through your mind as you're presenting these days?

My story matters. I can help someone today. Think about all the speeches that have made a difference to you in your life - you can do this for someone else right now. Be yourself. Be real. Tell the truth. Have fun.

What tips would you give to new speakers? Does it get easier? How did it get easier for you?

It really does get easier. While nervousness may never fully go away, I have found that nervousness often means you're about to grow, and that you're about to do something important. The very few times I didn't feel nervous before a speech, it was because I was way too deep in my comfort zone. Those were the times I knew it was time for the next challenge. Nervousness is a good thing. The only people who never feel nervous are those who never grow.

What last piece of advice would you impart to new speakers?

Talking about yourself in a speech is not going to turn people off. What people find most entertaining is true stories, especially personal stories that relate to your topic, stories only you know, stories only people who know you would know. That is something special. That is a gift. Give that gift to your audience and they will love you and applaud you every single time. Be honest. Be authentic. We need more of that, and a speech is always an opportunity to give a little of yourself to the people watching you.

You'd be surprised how much you can impact them with your stories, your heart, your life, when shared authentically. A great speaker cares more about the audience getting something out of it than about how they're perceived. Let that take the pressure off. Who you are is enough, and people will love you for being you. I promise.

Instructor, Media Coach, Workshop Facilitator, MA

How long have you been presenting/performing as part of your job?

As a college student, I was a tour guide at Disney's Hollywood studios, where I'd perform for groups of 200 people at a time! My first real job in the communication business was as a morning radio co-host and news director in 1995. I'd start each day at 4:00 am, reading the wires and writing stories to include in our broadcast. I'd be on-air for 5 hours, 5 days a week. By the time I was done at 10:00 am, I didn't want to talk to anyone.

How often do you have to present in front of a crowd?

Constantly!

How big are the audiences you present in front of?

15-500

How did you feel as a high school or college student giving speeches in class? Describe what went through your head and what you felt when you were assigned a speech, once you were preparing, the day of the speech, and once you were speaking.

That was 100 years ago - I can't even remember it! I think I just did what I had to do. I don't remember loving or hating it.

How do you feel now as someone who gives speeches for a living or as part of your job? Describe what goes through your head and what do you feel like when you get a speaking gig, once you're preparing, the day of the speech, and once you start speaking.

I get nervous just like everyone else. The less prepared I am, the more anxious I get. I never agree to speak on a topic that I'm not an absolute expert on. Even if I'm knowledgeable on a subject, I need to feel like I know more than anyone else in the room. I hate the thought of wasting anyone's time.

How did you make progress from the time you were a student to now? What did you do to improve as a speaker?

Even 20 years after graduating college, I'm constantly refining my technique. In the beginning, I worried most about things like delivery and gestures. As I've gotten older, my focus has switched to audience engagement.

What did you do to increase your confidence?

I wish I could say I had some trick or new idea, but the fact of the matter is that nothing boosts confidence like preparation. I don't even mean rehearsing - I mean being entirely comfortable with the subject and the order of information.

What do you do to stay in the moment and enjoy your time presenting in front of a crowd?

I'm happiest when I can see the audience is involved and interested - asking questions, giving opinions.

What positive thoughts go through your mind as you're presenting these days?

Honestly, I'm not thinking about the act of presenting while I'm presenting. I'm most in the moment when I'm focused on the content itself. To try to remind myself of anything (even if the intent is to inspire or pump myself up) would just be a distraction and one more thing to remember.

What tips would you give to new speakers? Does it get easier? How did it get easier for you?

As with anything, the more you do it, the better you will be. There's just no way around the fact that experience is the best teacher. If you feel like your delivery is weak, focus on the organization of the speech (and the content) to feel more confident. If you're naturally dynamic, don't disregard the need for preparation. No matter how charismatic you are, people can tell when you have not prepared. Often disorganization gives it away. Nobody likes a speech that bounces around and nobody likes a story that goes nowhere. People will remember your speech long after you present it. Give it the time and effort it deserves

Speakers in Professional Consulting

<u>Human Communication Consultant, Instructor, Speaker, Coach, MA</u>

How long have you been presenting/performing as part of your job?

I started my professional career 15 years ago and continually found myself in a position to speak, whether it was motivating a group of athletes while I was coaching, or as a corporate trainer for marketing, leasing, and technical software. I've been presenting for 15 years now, and specifically teaching public speaking for 7 years.

How often do you have to present in front of a crowd?

In my current job position, I present 3 to 4 days each week in front a crowd.

How big are the audiences you present in front of?

When I'm working at the university, my smallest class size is 30 students. The largest is 300. For consulting work though, I speak to much smaller groups... usually around 5-10 employees.

How did you feel as a high school or college student giving speeches in class? Describe what went through your head and what you felt when you were assigned a speech, once you were preparing, the day of the speech, and once you were speaking.

Honestly, I always enjoyed giving speeches. Of course I would be nervous, but it was more about excitement than about fear. I like being a voice for topics that I think are important.

When I was assigned a speech, the most difficult thing was deciding what I wanted to speak about. And I wondered how I would fill the time. I was a diligent student, though, and would prepare my speeches way ahead of the due date so that I could have time to revise it and practice it many times. And I did practice a lot. In high school and college, I would focus on remembering what I wanted to say as I was much more scripted at that time and was good at memorizing speeches. It wasn't until I became older and more experienced that I became a good extemporaneous speaker.

How do you feel now as someone who gives speeches for a living or as part of your job? Describe what goes through your head and what do you feel like when you get a speaking gig, once you're preparing, the day of the speech, and once you start speaking.

I love speaking and would much rather be the one up in front of the crowd than sitting in the audience. When I have a speaking gig these days, I first think of who will be in my audience and what they might expect to hear from me. Then I decide how I will take the topic and make it relevant to the audience while still accomplishing what I want with the speech. To prepare, I always start with a rough outline. I just jot down talking points with pen and paper in order to have a structure to think about and then refine. After that, I think about what credible sources (other than myself) that I can include in the speech. Once I start speaking, I think about connecting with the audience. I want there to be a human interaction that's going on between me and the people in the room. I want there to be a palpable exchange of energy between us. I tell the audience my name and thank them for the opportunity to be with them for the speech. I give my energy to them through my interaction.

How did you make progress from the time you were a student to now? What did you do to improve as a speaker?

I made progress from taking every opportunity to speak. It's the old trial-and-error method. I'd speak, make some mistakes, get feedback, and implement the feedback the next time I spoke. I also made sure to use clear structure with writing and delivering speeches. It helps me and the audience to have this structure to follow.

What did you do to increase your confidence?

My confidence comes from my knowledge. I won't speak about something I'm not qualified for. What would be the point? What value would I be offering to the audience? When I know that I have important information to share and that I have good communication skills to make the audience understand this information, then I'm confident while speaking. I know that my audience will walk away from our time together having gained something of value.

What do you do to stay in the moment and enjoy your time presenting in front of a crowd?

To stay in the moment, I interact with the audience. I like talking with people and this is my style of speaking... it's much more conversational than lecture-like.

What positive thoughts go through your mind as you're presenting these days?

I think about the connections that I probably will make with some people in the audience. Several audience members will likely approach me after the speech to introduce themselves and share their personal stories with me. I love this kind of human interaction. For me, it's the reward for speaking.

What tips would you give to new speakers? Does it get easier? How did it get easier for you?

My first tip is to take every chance to speak that you can get. If you're in a meeting and have a question, stand up to ask it at the appropriate time. Get used to being seen and heard. Enjoy using your voice. The more you practice, the easier it can get. You have to be willing to make mistakes and then fix them for the future.

The second tip is to remember that the speech isn't about you the speaker. We are often very egocentric and think about ourselves. Instead, realize that as the speaker you have a job and you're there not for yourself but to serve your audience. You know something important and you need them to know it, too. So you have a job to do and this job is about helping others, not about you.

What last piece of advice would you impart to new speakers?

If you're experiencing fear of public speaking, realize that this fear is often irrational. Your body is reacting to perceived danger, but the reality is that you're not in danger. It's just your perception of the situation that is creating your fearful response. You have the power to reshape your perspectives. You don't have to be afraid to speak. You can be in control.

<u>Independent Educational Consultant, Writer/Speaker, and retired</u>
<u>teacher</u>

How long have you been presenting/performing as part of your job?

I have been doing this for 40+ years

How often do you have to present in front of a crowd?

Currently, around 8-10 times a year

How big are the audiences you present in front of?

Anywhere from 10 to 900 (a joint meeting of the Southern and Potomac & Chesapeake College Admissions Associations)

How did you feel as a high school or college student giving speeches in class? Describe what went through your head and what you felt when you were assigned a speech, once you were preparing, the day of the speech, and once you were speaking.

There was almost always a sense of "Will this be okay?" A big help to me was being in the high school glee club, which required singing before a group. Speeches, of course, are different, and depending on the setting I was usually moderately composed. Curiously, the more unfamiliar the audience, the more comfortable I was.

How do you feel now as someone who gives speeches for a living or as part of your job? Describe what goes through your head and what do you feel like when you get a speaking gig, once you're preparing, the day of the speech, and once you start speaking.

There is usually a favorable anticipation for giving a speech. Something about 'being onstage' is a good thing. I genuinely enjoy speaking before a group.

How did you make progress from the time you were a student to now? What did you do to improve as a speaker?

Experience is the best teacher, and usually we aren't consciously gauging our growth, it evolves. For me, it's easier to seem as if I am delivering my comments by heart rather than reading them. Losing my place as a reader was/is far more disconcerting than appearing to be speaking off the cuff. This suggests that I am familiar with my topic to the degree that a few notes to keep me on track are all I have in front of me.

What did you do to increase your confidence?

It is almost always true that establishing a rapport with the audience right away, usually with some humor or conveying a friendly demeanor, is a guarantee that it will be a successful experience. On occasion, I have surprised the audience by opening with song- maybe just a line or two- that relates to the topic or the situation. For example, at a graduation speech recently, I began by singing the first stanza of the Louis Armstrong song, "What a Wonderful World" and then led into my speech which was centered on how these graduates would make it an even more wonderful world.

What do you do to stay in the moment and enjoy your time presenting in front of a crowd?

I balance the light with the serious.

What positive thoughts go through your mind as you're presenting these days?

Candidly, I simply live in the moment and enjoy sharing something I know with an audience, which I presume has a sense of why I am there.

What tips would you give to new speakers? Does it get easier? How did it get easier for you?

I think much of what I have written above speaks to this question.

What last piece of advice would you impart to new speakers?

Convey your own personality; if you flub something, laugh it off. If you want to address the elephant in the room, say at the beginning that you know a mistake will probably make them more uncomfortable than it does you, so they needn't worry on your behalf.

Speakers in Ministry

<u>Student Ministry Director</u>

Other side projects/jobs that include presenting/performing:

Camp & Conference Speaker

How long have you been presenting/performing as part of your job?

10+ years.

How often do you have to present in front of a crowd?

At least twice weekly. Sometimes considerably more.

How big are the audiences you present in front of?

Audiences range from 20-30 in a classroom, to an average of 600 students at our midweek service, to as many as 2,500 in a single weekend service.

How did you feel as a high school or college student giving speeches in class? Describe what went through your head and what you felt when you were assigned a speech, once you were preparing, the day of the speech, and once you were speaking.

I would get anxious about the upcoming speech. I was always fairly comfortable with my content, but it was the delivery. I would get very red when I had to speak in front of groups.

How do you feel now as someone who gives speeches for a living or as part of your job? Describe what goes through your head and what do you feel like when you get a speaking gig, once you're preparing, the day of the speech, and once you start speaking.

I always feel a certain amount of nervousness, especially if it is a paid opportunity. I want to make an impact, and I want to meet people's expectations. So I feel the weight of that. I prepare as much as I can, ask a lot of questions about the intended audience, and I do quite a bit of praying. That for me is what makes the difference.

How did you make progress from the time you were a student to now? What did you do to improve as a speaker?

I read a ton of books on communication:
Everyone Communicates, Few Connect: What the Most Effective People Do Differently by John C. Maxwell
Made to Stick: Why Some Ideas Survive and Others Die by Chip Heath & Dan Heath
Communicating for a Change: Seven Keys to Irresistible Communication by Andy Stanley & Lane Jones

I watched, studied, and learned from as many communicators as I could. I consistently videotape myself and watch it back. I also ask others for feedback on content and delivery. Inviting open and honest feedback is the thing that has pushed me to where I am.

What did you do to increase your confidence?

I was overly prepared and got in as many rehearsals as I could. I took advantage of any and every opportunity.

What do you do to stay in the moment and enjoy your time presenting in front of a crowd?

To me, you have to have crowd interaction to be a great communicator. Giving a speech is one thing. Anyone can transfer information. But when you engage a crowd, create a moment with them, feel something together, move them towards change, that's what I'm after. I try to tell stories, read the audience, and ask questions.

What positive thoughts go through your mind as you're presenting these days?

I'm to the point where I really enjoy what I do. There are certainly occasions where I don't feel like I'm connecting and some of my thoughts might be negative, but for the most part I just think about what an incredible opportunity it is to be able to influence others.

What tips would you give to new speakers? Does it get easier? How did it get easier for you?

It absolutely gets easier. I would tell new speakers that there is no opportunity too small. We communicate with people every day thousands of times a day; each of those interactions as a learning opportunity. I think most new speakers try to do too much too soon. If you're new I would say: Be brief, be brilliant, be gone. It's better to be amazing for 10 minutes than decent for 40. Find 10 different communicators and highlight the best one or two things that each of them do, then try to integrate it into the way you do things. At the same time, don't worry about being someone else. Just be yourself. I think that's rule number one for audience engagement. You have to believe what you're selling.

Speakers in Business

<u>Contracts Negotiator for Lockheed Martin, MBA</u>

How long have you been presenting/performing as part of your job?

18 months

How often do you have to present in front of a crowd?

Once a month

How big are the audiences you present in front of?

Between 10 and 100+ people

How did you feel as a high school or college student giving speeches in class? Describe what went through your head and what you felt when you were assigned a speech, once you were preparing, the day of the speech, and once you were speaking.

I was petrified of public speaking. I avoided it at all costs. In college when I was forced to take public speaking, I got physically ill before the first day of class. By the last speech of the term my speech teacher told me I had given the "best speech she'd ever heard" and I was almost instantly relieved of my fear.

How do you feel now as someone who gives speeches for a living or as part of your job? Describe what goes through your head and what do you feel like when you get a speaking gig, once you're preparing, the day of the speech, and once you start speaking.

Public speaking is not my favorite. However, my nerves are channeled in a positive way. And I must say there are not many thrills like giving a great presentation in front of a crowd.

How did you make progress from the time you were a student to now? What did you do to improve as a speaker?

I practiced my speeches at least 20 times before I gave them in front of the class. As long as I was familiar with the content (even if it was memorized), it was one less thing I had to worry about. I could focus on eye contact and gestures and engaging the audience.

What did you do to increase your confidence?

Practice in front of family and friends. I let them give me their opinion and make changes to my presentation to better suit an audience.

What do you do to stay in the moment and enjoy your time presenting in front of a crowd?

I like to ask questions and, when it's appropriate, make some jokes to ease the crowd.

What positive thoughts go through your mind as you're presenting these days?

I just replay what my speech teacher in college said to me after my final presentation. It's quite the compliment knowing I gave the best speech she had ever heard.

What tips would you give to new speakers? Does it get easier? How did it get easier for you?

As much as you may hate public speaking, the more you do it the better you get. I hated hearing that from dad, but it's true.

What last piece of advice would you impart to new speakers?

Practice and know your content.

Speakers in College Administration

Director of the School of Professional and Career Education for a private university; Instructor and Lecturer for Diversity in the Workplace

How long have you been presenting/performing as part of your job?

18 years

How often do you have to present in front of a crowd?

At least once a month

How big are the audiences you present in front of?

It ranges from 6 to 300 people

How did you feel as a high school or college student giving speeches in class? Describe what went through your head and what you felt when you were assigned a speech, once you were preparing, the day of the speech, and once you were speaking.

I was always very excited for speech class. I was never very good at sports or anything athletic, so as a "boy" I felt inadequate at times as a result of this. However, I knew that if placed in front of an audience, I was able to wield effort to deliver a good performance. I found self-value and confidence in this ability. The preparation process was always fun, because it was a creative phase of the presentation that gave me the opportunity to construct my delivery of the speech.

The day of the speech, regardless of the amount of time I spent preparing, I was always extremely anxious and nervous. The nervous energy was not associated with a lack of confidence in my ability to do well, but because of it. I know this is a paradox, but the passion for doing a great job manifested into nervous energy that would build up until the very moment I was called to the front of the audience. Once I was center stage delivering the speech, all of the nervous energy worked in my favor. I was always able to harness and channel that energy into my execution and delivery of the message.

How do you feel now as someone who gives speeches for a living or as part of your job? Describe what goes through your head and what do you feel like when you get a speaking gig, once you're preparing, the day of the speech, and once you start speaking.

Today I continue to feel exhilarated with the prospect of delivering a message as one component of the essential functions of my job. When provided a speaking gig, I immediately feel excited, thrilled, and nervous all at once. The next notion in my mind is the preparation I need to do for the targeted audience. Within moments of receiving the assignment, my mind is already envisioning a finished product. The preparation process remains a creative, almost artistic one because I not only consider the facts to be presented, the audience I am presenting to, but I also incorporate different delivery methods to maximize the effectiveness and impact of the speech.

The day of the speech I am always excited and, yes, still quite nervous. But just as before, once I begin delivering the speech, the nervous energy is always perceived by others and the audience as passion for the subject matter and infused in my delivery style.

How did you make progress from the time you were a student to now? What did you do to improve as a speaker?

The progress definitely came from experience. The more speaking engagements I participated in, the more comfortable I became with the process of preparation and delivery. My method of improvement in my oratorical skills was to study the craft in order to hone it. I was sure to incorporate communication into my undergraduate and graduate degrees.

What did you do to increase your confidence?

Rehearse. There is no better tool to increase confidence in giving speeches, than rehearsing it.

What do you do to stay in the moment and enjoy your time presenting in front of a crowd?

For me it is all about the connection you feel with your audience. It has to be a visceral experience where you are taking your audience on a ride. Knowing that I'm the facilitator of the audience's experience is how I sustain enjoyment and gratification in the experience.

What positive thoughts go through your mind as you're presenting these days?

I remind myself that 99.9%, if not the entire audience, is always rooting for you. Always. People, for the most part, will always want you to succeed and do well. That reassurance and the energy the audience emits can lift you up in the speech giving experience.

What tips would you give to new speakers? Does it get easier? How did it get easier for you?

Rehearse. Rehearse. Rehearse. There is no better tool. Yes, with rehearsals, and over time, the experience does get easier and always a lot more fun. It became easier for me the more I practiced doing it.

What last piece of advice would you impart to new speakers?

Be passionate about what you do. You have to believe in your subject matter. My last piece of advice is, no matter what subject you are asked to speak on, find something about the topic that inspires you, that makes you feel good. This connection with it will elevate your performance to optimal levels. And finally, I can't say this enough: rehearse, rehearse, rehearse.

<u>Dean of Communication for a Florida college</u>

How long have you been presenting/performing as part of your job?

20 years

How often do you have to present in front of a crowd?

About once a month for the past five years

How big are the audiences you present in front of?

Under 40

How did you feel as a high school or college student giving speeches in class? Describe what went through your head and what you felt when you were assigned a speech, once you were preparing, the day of the speech, and once you were speaking.

I don't think I minded giving presentations in class, although they always came with the same flutters. I had an overconfidence combined with procrastination, so I only prepared the night before the presentation, and then rarely practiced. That meant that when I gave the presentation, I stumbled and did not provide a smooth presentation. I practiced more when I was performing a solo in chorus, and my nerves were much greater when singing than when speaking.

How do you feel now as someone who gives speeches for a living or as part of your job? Describe what goes through your head and what do you feel like when you get a speaking gig, once you're preparing, the day of the speech, and once you start speaking.

Unfortunately, I suffer from social anxiety, so while presentations are not my favorite, I find them much easier to give than speaking in a group of peers. I prepare an agenda for my presentations and know what I'm going to say, so that takes most of the anxiety out of it. When I'm speaking, I try to remember to be aware of my body language and to maintain eye contact with the audience.

How did you make progress from the time you were a student to now? What did you do to improve as a speaker?

When I first started as a student teacher, I was so nervous about speaking to students that I would write down everything I was going to say, and then write down what I thought the students' response would be, and then write down what I would say next. I over prepared my materials, and that put me more at ease. I knew I wouldn't have to guess. Now, I don't feel like I have to write everything down, but I do make notes of speaking points.

What did you do to increase your confidence?

To increase my confidence, I thought through the entire presentation and visualized success. For one keynote address I had to make a few years ago, I practiced by giving it to my students first to get their feedback.

What do you do to stay in the moment and enjoy your time presenting in front of a crowd?

I try to take me out of the equation and focus on the audience — what I can do to make them more engaged with the subject? It's a unique kind of energy to feed off of.

What positive thoughts go through your mind as you're presenting these days?

When I'm speaking, I tend to smile. Also, I've always had compliments on the sound of my voice. I keep these things in mind while I'm convincing myself that the audience likes me!

What tips would you give to new speakers? Does it get easier? How did it get easier for you?

The best tip I can give is that procrastination is not your friend. Preparing in advance and then practicing will make the presentation go much more smoothly.

What last piece of advice would you impart to new speakers?

One of my students was giving a presentation one day, all dressed up (she was normally a sweatsuit kind of girl). She got so nervous that she started to cry and ran out of the room. After I went after her to calm her down, all it took was for her to take off her heels for her to come back in and complete the presentation. Sometimes just a touch of added anxiety will push you to paralysis. Use mindful meditation and positive self-talk, and avoid heels at all costs!

<u>Assistant Director of Communication Arts Online at a Florida university</u>

Other side projects/jobs that include presenting/performing:

VTCOA (Viper Truck Club of America)

How long have you been presenting/performing as part of your job?

3 years

How often do you have to present in front of a crowd?

Generally about 2-3 times per semester (once every 2 months about)

How big are the audiences you present in front of?

Small groups of about 15-30 employees or faculty members

How did you feel as a high school or college student giving speeches in class? Describe what went through your head and what you felt when you were assigned a speech, once you were preparing, the day of the speech, and once you were speaking.

Anytime you are required to give a speech, nerves will radiate through your body. This is normal! Just as an athlete prepares for a game/match, a speaker must prepare mentally for their part. The key to giving a speech is to just go up and do it. You cannot worry about messing up or having stage fright, you have to just muster up the courage and go. The longer you wait, the more anxiety you will feel. Nobody is perfect and your audience knows that, so just go up there and give it your all!

How do you feel now as someone who gives speeches for a living or as part of your job? Describe what goes through your head and what do you feel like when you get a speaking gig, once you're preparing, the day of the speech, and once you start speaking.

Now out of my athletic prime (actually, come to think of it, I may not have ever had a prime!), I see public speaking as the same kind of rush that preparing for a sporting event gave me. It is normal to get nervous and anxious to speak, but transfer those nerves into production! Once you are up at the podium or in front of your crowd, and you get going, you will forget about why you were even nervous in the first place.

How did you make progress from the time you were a student to now? What did you do to improve as a speaker?

Practice. Practice. And more practice. Never back down on the opportunity to speak in front of people. The more you do it, the more comfortable you will be. I even recommend going first when you have to give a speech, this way you set the tone and learn to take charge when it comes to the daunting task of public speaking.

What did you do to increase your confidence?

To increase my confidence, I make sure that I am in the right mindset. It is normal to be nervous, but make sure that you do not allow your nerves to take control of how you speak. If you know the material, then you can just go up and talk as if you are speaking to your friends. You are up there for a reason, so your audience will listen to what you have to say!

What do you do to stay in the moment and enjoy your time presenting in front of a crowd?

Know that you are not perfect, nor is anybody in the audience. If you make a mistake, then just pause, reset, and continue to grace your audience with your voice and knowledge!

What positive thoughts go through your mind as you're presenting these days?

As my father used to say, "Go get em tiger…"

What tips would you give to new speakers? Does it get easier? How did it get easier for you?

As with anything new, it takes practice to get better. Of course it will get easier, but you will always get the same nerves you got the first time you did it. The key, as stated before, is to convert those nerves into confidence!

What last piece of advice would you impart to new speakers?

Paul Arden once said, "Too many people spend too much time trying to perfect something before they actually do it. Instead of waiting for perfection, run with what you got, and fix it along the way…" With that end, go enlighten the world with what you know and if you should hit a roadblock, just come up with solutions rather than a panic.

Executive Director of Alumni Engagement for a private university

How long have you been presenting/performing as part of your job?

I began my professional career in 1987, but have only been making presentations since 1992. I spent those first 5 years strategically making sure I would not have to give a presentation because I was deathly afraid to do so! True story.

How often do you have to present in front of a crowd?

My current position requires me to give presentations to multiple groups on a very regular basis, and I've presented on many different topics over the years. The list includes:
-Board of Trustees meetings
-Alumni events
-Planning for college workshops (I've done over 100 of these with groups that have ranged from 15 to 500 people)
-Juvenile Diabetes Research Foundation (JDRF) Corporate Luncheons
-Admissions Presentations (I've done several thousand of these)
-Campus tours
-Panels at national conferences
-Staff meetings
-Media interviews (which scare me to death, but I actually enjoy doing them)
-Radio

How big are the audiences you present in front of?

It ranges from 1 to 1800 people.

How did you feel as a high school or college student giving speeches in class? Describe what went through your head and what you felt when you were assigned a speech, once you were preparing, the day of the speech, and once you were speaking.

As I said earlier, I avoided having to make presentations at all costs for the first 25 years of my life. There was only one presentation that I remember making in college, and it was basically presenting a paper I had to write for my religion class. The paper was on perceptions created and reaffirmed by the media, which in the early 80's, was vastly different than what we have today. I didn't practice it, but apparently I wrote it in a way that, when presented, was kind of humorous, in a good way. Getting that positive reaction from the class helped me get through the remainder of the presentation.

How do you feel now as someone who gives speeches for a living or as part of your job? Describe what goes through your head and what do you feel like when you get a speaking gig, once you're preparing, the day of the speech, and once you start speaking.

This is not advice that I would give anyone, but my best, most effective speeches are written the morning of the event. Crazy right? So whenever I would be presenting at a student recruitment/admissions open house, I would have the notes from the previous year. However, the morning of, I typically come in early and run through it, editing the document to try to make it as pertinent and appropriate as possible, so that I go into the presentation having just presented it to myself numerous times.

Many times when I am making a presentation, I am not behind a podium, but rather just standing in front of a crowd, and even sometimes in the middle of a room, with people 360 degrees around me. That's tough. I've even gotten dizzy as I circled around addressing everyone. My presentation style, I've been told is very conversational, versus "giving a presentation." I approach it as if I am having a one-way conversation with the audience, whether it is 5 or 500 people. I've been told that I seem genuine when I am presenting, which is awesome because I actually am.

To be able to "believe in" what you are talking about, makes it much easier.

Sometimes I will pick out a certain audience member who unwisely chose to sit on the front row where I could make eye contact with them, and to engage them in your presentation sometimes helps your overall speech to be conversational to the group as a whole. I am always aware of my facial expressions whenever giving a presentation. Smiling at the appropriate time I think helps others to smile with you, which in a sense offers approval and belief in what you have just stated. What to do with your hands is also something I am conscious of. If you have a podium, that makes it much, much easier. If you don't have a podium, you just want to make sure you find a happy medium between how a coach or manager gives baseball signs to the runners and batters, to having your arms straight down by your side or in your pockets.

You want your audience to hear what you are saying, and not be distracted by "how you are saying it" or letting the motions of your hands, arms, legs, feet, etc. compete with the subject matter you are presenting.

How did you make progress from the time you were a student to now? What did you do to improve as a speaker?

Practice, Practice, Practice. I practice by myself, but also in front of groups. You also need to realize that most people in the audience are so happy they are not you, and would generally never look for opportunities to have to put themselves in the a position like that, so you're kind of doing something incredible.

What did you do to increase your confidence?

I know I am my own worst and biggest critic. I think if I weren't, I would be a pretty bad presenter. I was talking to my wife a while back, and it was after a presentation where I definitely did not feel like I met the expectations that were set for me. She told me that just because I didn't receive a standing ovation, didn't mean it was a horrible speech. She also said it's not realistic to think that you are going to walk away on cloud nine, after every presentation. That's the goal, but you start to realize that it's not going to happen like that every time, and it's absolutely okay. That talk actually increased my confidence for future presentation; it took some pressure off.

What do you do to stay in the moment and enjoy your time presenting in front of a crowd?

I think it goes back to it being a performance. You need to be able to present your material in a genuine, interesting, relative and truthful way. Knowing that helps me to stay present with the audience, because I want to make valuable use of their time.

What positive thoughts go through your mind as you're presenting these days?

At this point in my career, I'm genuinely excited about and believe in the presentations that I'm expected to give, and I hope to provide value to those I'm able to interact with. I'm still nervous, but I feel like I have an important purpose in being there.

What tips would you give to new speakers? Does it get easier? How did it get easier for you?

I really view presentations as a performance, a form of entertainment, and not that you have to try and be a comedian to entertain, but you are basically putting on a show in delivering the information for that specific occasion. You need to figure out how to laugh at yourself when it comes to making presentations, because it's much more fun to laugh with people about something than just be laughed at! I regret never taking a public speaking class, or waiting so long before realizing that I was going to have to make presentations in my chosen profession. I still get nervous every time I go on stage or get in front of a group. I typically don't like to have to be chatty with anyone prior to beginning a presentation, because I need time to focus on what I am getting ready to say, especially the first few words and sentences. Through practice, having to present for crowds has gotten easier.

What last piece of advice would you impart to new speakers?

Just know that if you are in a position where you are going to have to present as part of your job or career, that the more you help yourself get the confidence and foundation of knowing how to pull it off successfully, the more successful you are going to be. The point of presentations is not to get people to like you, but rather to like the information you are presenting. And know that you are in the majority of people in this world... who would rather be actually lying in the casket, versus standing at the podium giving the eulogy.

<u>Advisor and College Student</u>

Other side projects/jobs that include presenting/performing:

I speak in various college classrooms about my academic career, and I give the occasional presentation at treatment centers throughout the US for those suffering from eating disorders.

How long have you been presenting/performing as part of your job?

Advisor: 1 year; College Student: 3 years

How often do you have to present in front of a crowd?

At least 3 to 4 times a month.

How big are the audiences you present in front of?

Each audience varies between 10-75 people/students depending on what I am presenting for.

How did you feel as a high school or college student giving speeches in class? Describe what went through your head and what you felt when you were assigned a speech, once you were preparing, the day of the speech, and once you were speaking.

I was very confident when it came to public speaking when I was in high school, and then the nerves came as I entered college. I went to a small private school for high school, so I knew most of the people I was presenting to. Once I got to college, the nerves started to kick in because I didn't know a single soul. I took speech my freshman year of college and would rush through most of my speeches in the beginning. However, once I became more comfortable and learned different techniques to calm myself down, I began to enjoy public speaking.

How do you feel now as someone who gives speeches for a living or as part of your job? Describe what goes through your head and what do you feel like when you get a speaking gig, once you're preparing, the day of the speech, and once you start speaking.

Before every speech or presentation, I still get a bit nervous (especially if it has been awhile since I have talked about a specific topic). When I get a speaking gig, I become very excited about the upcoming endeavor. Once I start preparing, I become somewhat critical of myself and then the nerves kick in, but not as bad as when the day of the speech actually arrives. The day of the speech, before I even start speaking, I am super nervous. However, the nerves seem to go away once I start to speak.

How did you make progress from the time you were a student to now? What did you do to improve as a speaker?

I am a natural born perfectionist, so no matter what I am doing, it must be performed to a "T." Though I am still young, I believe that over the years I have gained confidence that has helped me achieved better public speaking skills. I also believe that because of the many speeches and presentations I have given since my freshman speech class, practice has done me well. Each time I speak, no matter what the subject may be, it will always be a learning experience.

Though I have been speaking for a few years now, I still get worked up like everyone and need to calm myself down. I have learned that people are interested in what I have to say, and if I carry myself in a way where I believe that, I will get my message across better and I will be more confident. I now take a step back, before and after every speech, to address the situation and how I am feeling. I have realized that it is not worth it to beat myself up over a silly talk; everyone gets nervous.

What did you do to increase your confidence?

Lots of practice in front of the mirror and then in front of family and friends. I know that I need to hold my shoulders back and have my head held high in order to speak with confidence. I know it may sound silly, but changing your posture really does make a difference. I also fought my inner perfectionist demon. This doesn't mean that I became a slacker, I just starting telling myself that it was okay to not be perfect 100% of the time.

What do you do to stay in the moment and enjoy your time presenting in front of a crowd?

When I'm presenting and I feel that I'm drifting off, I use my 5 senses to stay in the moment. I usually focus the most on sight, by making eye contact to try and stay connected with the audience. I talk to myself (in my head, of course) to remind myself that I am doing a good job, and so that I can focus on getting an effective message across to the audience.

What positive thoughts go through your mind as you're presenting these days?

When I am presenting (mainly for work), I remind myself that I am making a difference in the lives of the students. Knowing that I can make an impact in at least one student's life helps me stay in the moment and enjoy my time presenting.

What tips would you give to new speakers? Does it get easier? How did it get easier for you?

Because I have always been a perfectionist, I would tell a new speaker to not beat themselves up over things. We will all make mistakes in speeches, even those who have been presenting their whole lives. It does get easier over time with practice and added self-confidence. If you believe that you can do it, you will.

What last piece of advice would you impart to new speakers?

There is always someone listening in your audience. Don't let the immature folks bring you down. You are impacting those who are there to listen to what you have to say because what you have to say is important.

Speakers in Education

Erin Lovell Ebanks
Communication and Public Speaking Instructor, Author, MA

Other side projects/jobs that include presenting/performing:

Musical performances for the occasional open mic night

How long have you been presenting as part of your job?

6 years

How often do you have to present in front of a crowd?

Nearly every class period in front of my students.

How big are the audiences you present in front of?

Around 30 people.

How did you feel as a high school or college student giving speeches in class? Describe what went through your head and what you felt when you were assigned a speech, once you were preparing, the day of the speech, and once you were speaking.

I was incredibly scared as a high school speaker, but a little more confident as a college speaker. I would get that surge of adrenaline as soon as the speech was assigned, but I always worked ahead and practiced a lot in front of friends and family because it eased my nerves leading up to the big day. I'm sure different calming techniques work for different people, but tons of preparation and practice was the best way for me to relax and feel good about the upcoming speech.

How do you feel now as someone who gives speeches for a living or as part of your job? Describe what goes through your head and what do you feel like when you get a speaking gig, once you're preparing, the day of the speech, and once you start speaking.

I still get a little adrenaline rush when I start lecturing, but it just energizes me enough to have fun with my students and maintain my enthusiasm throughout our discussion. I've done the same lectures and have become so familiar with communication concepts, that I feel very comfortable speaking about them as an expert, and I can have more fun with the material. I always interact with the audience, and use specific examples that they've shared during the term to keep them engaged. I'll probably try some different lectures next term, and possibly facilitate some public speaking workshops, which will be a new experience. I've become very comfortable lecturing in my own classrooms. I have the skills now to move beyond the classroom and get a taste of what my new speech students feel each semester as beginners. It might be time for a new challenge to stretch myself.

How did you make progress from the time you were a student to now? What did you do to improve as a speaker?

I am much less nervous, I put less pressure on myself to present 'perfectly,' I have more fun as a speaker, and I feel more confident. I think some of that comes with age.

Throughout the years, I purposefully put myself in uncomfortable situations almost daily, and I put myself 'onstage' as much as possible to get better as a presenter/performer. I performed at open mic nights, sang in talent shows, tried out for plays, and gave teaching a try as a grad student. Every one of those scared me, but in the best way possible. In a way that caused continual growth. It was just about practicing and presenting frequently enough that performing and public speaking never became an insurmountable challenge. That practice and experience taught me how to handle my nerves and enjoy the moment.

What did you do to increase your confidence?

A lot of practice and positive self-talk. If I started internalizing negative thoughts- for me personally- it was debilitating. I always keep my inner monologue very positive; it's tremendously encouraging.

What do you do to stay in the moment and enjoy your time presenting in front of a crowd?

I kind of 'check myself' about a minute into my lectures. I want to be sure I'm having a good time and that my students are having a good time. I take note of how I'm feeling, how my students are responding, I remind myself to make meaningful eye contact with my students. I also get excited when they are interested in a concept that might be slightly confusing, but I've managed to make it engaging; I take note of how I did that so I can repeat it with other concepts in the future.

The best way to stay in the moment is to remember to smile, truly connect with the audience, and allow for plenty of laughter! Be genuine, and let the audience enjoy that.

What positive thoughts go through your mind as you're presenting these days?

Every time I lecture, I think to myself, "I still can't believe I did it. I overcame America's number one fear. I actually enjoy speaking in public. I have made a career out of this! This is so much fun; my students are laughing and answering my questions. This feels really effective. How can I do more of this?..." I enjoy acknowledging that I have done something most people are scared to do; it makes me very appreciative, and helps me maintain my enthusiasm for my job.

What tips would you give to new speakers? Does it get easier? How did it get easier for you?

It gets so much easier, but you need to keep practicing. It's easy to slip back into a comfort zone and let those fears re-emerge. If you keep putting yourself in the spotlight and developing your skills, you are going to have an exciting and opportunity-filled life ahead of you!

What last piece of advice would you impart to new speakers?

Fear is completely made up. Don't let it hold you back from showing people who you really are. Get a valuable message to your audience that you can be proud of.

<u>Adjunct Psychology Professor, MA</u>

Other side projects/jobs that include presenting/performing:

Career as an image consultant, served as an emcee for a fashion show, served as a speaker at a marriage retreat, president of a women's church group

How long have you been presenting/performing as part of your job?

I have been teaching at the college level off and on for nearly 45 years. In addition to teaching, I have had to use my public speaking skills in other careers and capacities.

How often do you have to present in front of a crowd?

When teaching in a semester, this could be 2-5 days per week, depending on the schedule.

How big are the audiences you present in front of?

Class enrollment is usually 25-32 students. I have spoken in front of other types of groups, such as clubs and fashion shows, with attendance ranging from 75-200.

How did you feel as a high school or college student giving speeches in class? Describe what went through your head and what you felt when you were assigned a speech, once you were preparing, the day of the speech, and once you were speaking.

That is so long ago for me, I honestly do not remember. I just remember doing some small things in front of the class in high school and knowing that I wanted to be a teacher.

How do you feel now as someone who gives speeches for a living or as part of your job? Describe what goes through your head and what do you feel like when you get a speaking gig,

once you're preparing, the day of the speech, and once you start speaking.

I try to prepare way in advance. I write an outline, practice in front of a mirror, while I am walking, and gesturing, and I time the speech. I try to relax, remember to smile, start off with something catchy/attention-getting, and then I just go with the flow.

How did you make progress from the time you were a student to now? What did you do to improve as a speaker?

There is much to be said for practice. Speaking about subject matter in my field of study, and for particular courses, is so well-rehearsed now; it makes it easy for me. The addition of technologies such as PowerPoint as background to one's talk or lecture, with short video clips added to punctuate, has been very liberating and has added to my effectiveness as an instructor.

What did you do to increase your confidence?

Practice, practice, practice.

What do you do to stay in the moment and enjoy your time presenting in front of a crowd?

I make sure I look at all sections of the audience, look people in the eye, walk from one side of the room to the other, ask questions, modulate my volume, insert humor where appropriate, and keep an eye on the clock.

What positive thoughts go through your mind as you're presenting these days?

Usually, these days, I do feel that "I am on" when lecturing in my field.

What tips would you give to new speakers? Does it get easier? How did it get easier for you?

Yes, it gets easier. However, I confess to my students on the first day of class in a new semester, that after all these years, I still get a little anxious about the first day, just like they do!

What last piece of advice would you impart to new speakers?

Again, practice, practice, practice. Also: know something about your audience, think of examples/things they can relate to, check out your technology in advance, check out the location in advance, be early for a speaking engagement rather than late or even on time, be respectful and stick to the time allotted, and leave time for questions!

Associate Professor of Communication and Media Studies

How long have you been presenting/performing as part of your job?

Since 1997 (18 years)

How often do you have to present in front of a crowd?

Daily

How big are the audiences you present in front of?

-University classes range from 12-20 students
-Faculty Senate meetings in front of 20 fellow faculty members
-Making points in university faculty meetings in front of about 50-125 people
-Research presentations at academic conferences usually about 15-20 people but in occasion have spoken in front of as many as 125 people (in the context of an invited lecture at another university)
-Reading scripture at Episcopal church as a lay reader in front of 100-200 people

How did you feel as a high school or college student giving speeches in class? Describe what went through your head and what you felt when you were assigned a speech, once you were preparing, the day of the speech, and once you were speaking.

I saw myself as a very shy, introverted person in high school and still somewhat in college, so I did not see getting up in front of a group as something I would want to seek out. I only did it if I absolutely had to for a grade or for an organization I was in; I would present if the sponsor asked me to do it. In college, I never took public speaking, though I did end up teaching many sections of it in the future. The strong point in my college presentations was that I always put much time into researching and thinking about the material.

I remember one Literary Criticism class, when I had to present on a literary theory, I brought the giant stack of books I had used with me, in case someone asked me a question and I needed to refer back to a source. Logistically, that would have been hard to do in the moment, but somehow it made me feel better knowing that I had all my books there with me, just in case. Having the books there may have boosted my credibility, as people could tell I had devoted energy into reading thoroughly on my topic. In many of my English major presentations, we presented from our seats in the circle of desks or chairs with the class, rather than standing in the front of the class. At the time, that made me feel less intimidated about speaking than if I had to stand in front of the classroom by myself. Several years later, I was telling one of my former English professors that I felt stronger as a writer than a speaker. I remember that he said I was a stronger speaker than I thought. I think back on that compliment from a professor, I very much respect and it gives me a confidence boost even today.

How do you feel now as someone who gives speeches for a living or as part of your job? Describe what goes through your head and what do you feel like when you get a speaking gig, once you're preparing, the day of the speech, and once you start speaking.

I do not see myself as someone who gives speeches for a living. I see myself as someone who communicates with people and leads discussions for a living. Even when presenting my research, I do not think of it as giving a speech, but more as sharing my research and ideas with others. This seems a less intimidating, more natural way of thinking about what I am doing.

How did you make progress from the time you were a student to now? What did you do to improve as a speaker?

The more I lead a class, share my research, speak in a meeting, or read the scriptures at my church, the more confident and comfortable I feel in those various speaking situations.

What did you do to increase your confidence?

The more familiar and knowledgeable I am with my content, the more at ease I feel about speaking. I have also learned not to over prepare and not to have too many written notes. If I think of speaking more as leading a discussion or conversation, that takes the pressure off in that I know I am trying to get others to participate along with me. I also try to remind myself, whether in teaching a class or giving a research presentation, that I probably have thought about the topic and read about it more extensively than the other people in the room, which helps me feel more confident, as well. They are there giving me their attention because they want me to share my knowledge and ideas with them so that they can add to their own knowledge of the topic.

What do you do to stay in the moment and enjoy your time presenting in front of a crowd?

When teaching class, I keep notes minimal and prefer to read the material the night before or earlier in the day before class so that it is very fresh in my mind. I have a somewhat photographic memory, so I can picture where the material is on the pages I read. I mark particular pages I may want to reference in the course of the class with Post-it notes, or I'll write the page numbers next to the points in my brief outline for the class. I send myself links to examples I want to show on the projector such as particular video clips or images.

Overall, I try to structure my classes as more of interactive discussions of the material. When I think of presenting in class as more like leading a discussion than giving a presentation, this makes me feel more at ease in front of the students. I want to come across as extemporaneous in my speaking, which is to say conversational, yet organized and prepared. I encourage my students to take a similar approach when they give class presentations.

<u>Public Speaking Instructor for a Florida college</u>

How long have you been presenting/performing as part of your job?

I started competing in statewide public speaking contests when I was in middle school, and I started acting in local plays when I was in elementary school. I always loved performing in front of an audience.

How often do you have to present in front of a crowd?

When I'm teaching, I am always speaking in front of my students.

How big are the audiences you present in front of?

I usually end up speaking in front of about 30 students at a time during classes, but large crowds don't bother me. I have spoken in front of an audience of over 4,000 people before I was even in high school.

How did you feel as a high school or college student giving speeches in class? Describe what went through your head and what you felt when you were assigned a speech, once you were preparing, the day of the speech, and once you were speaking.

I always felt comfortable speaking in front of the class in high school and college. I believe that the number one thing that helped me to feel comfortable when assigned a speech and preparing for it was to practice and know exactly what I needed and wanted to say. When I'm speaking now, I try to leave a little room for spontaneity and responding to the audience.

How do you feel now as someone who gives speeches for a living or as part of your job? Describe what goes through your head and what you feel like when you get a speaking gig, once you're preparing, the day of the speech, and once you start speaking.

My process has generally remained the same.

How did you make progress from the time you were a student to now? What did you do to improve as a speaker?

When I was younger and competing in public speaking contests, especially at the state level, it was all about perfection and memorizing a speech word for word. Now that I'm older, I realize that an emphasis on 'perfection,' or word for word delivery, doesn't always leave a lot of room for personality and engaging your audience. I now focus on getting across a message by interacting with the audience.

What did you do to increase your confidence?

In all honesty, public speaking is something that I have done from a very young age and have never felt a lack of confidence while doing it. However, I think it helps knowing that most of the time your audience is cheering for you rather than picking you apart. I also have years of improv theatre experience and learning how to respond instantly to the unexpected in front of an audience. That has proven to be a valuable skill.

What do you do to stay in the moment and enjoy your time presenting in front of a crowd?

I try to stay in the moment by engaging my audience and responding to their cues. For example, if my students are really surprised by something that is mentioned during a lecture, I try to expand on it. If my students seem to understand the content already, I don't feel it's necessary to spend more time than needed on something they already know.

What positive thoughts go through your mind as you're presenting these days?

When I'm presenting these days, usually I'm trying to help students learn new concepts. I love it when I can see students thinking about new ideas, and I really try to make my lectures engaging enough that I capture their attention.

What tips would you give to new speakers? Does it get easier? How did it get easier for you?

Practice always makes speaking easier. In today's world of communication through the use of technology, I don't think that people always get enough experience speaking in front of others. Taking advantage of opportunities to practice in front of a group are always helpful. Even if you don't have a group to practice in front of, practicing in front of the people around you is always beneficial. You just don't get the same feedback from practicing by yourself as you do from practicing in front of live humans.

What last piece of advice would you impart to new speakers?

Be prepared. Practice. Don't procrastinate. Know how you want things to go, but don't be afraid of spontaneity. Sometimes live performances take an unexpected turn and those moments can be some of the most interesting to an audience. If you are nervous, it never hurts to pretend to be confident. Don't try to imitate another person's speaking style. You have to find what works best for you, and that allows you to leave a little bit of yourself in each presentation.

Professor of Speech, Keiser University; Adjunct Professor, Stetson University

Other side projects/jobs that include presenting/performing:

I have been in a leadership position with the American Civil Liberties Union (ACLU) for about a dozen years or so, so I am often a guest speaker or panel member on political issues. I also speak to county council and city commission meetings, school boards, etc. Public speaking workshops pop up along the way, as well.

How long have you been presenting/performing as part of your job?

I started teaching college classes while still a Graduate Assistant in the late '70's, but I taught my first college classes as an adjunct instructor in 1985 and have been teaching ever since.

How often do you have to present in front of a crowd?

As a college teacher, I have to present daily, year-round. Outside of my job, I probably speak to crowds every other month or so.

How big are the audiences you present in front of?

My classes average is about 20 – 25 students. Outside audiences range from small groups to several hundred.

How did you feel as a high school or college student giving speeches in class? Describe what went through your head and what you felt when you were assigned a speech, once you were preparing, the day of the speech, and once you were speaking.

As a student, I was scared to death, just like everyone else. But as I got more and more prepared, my confidence grew. After a while, I realized I could actually DO this stuff, and it gave me a feeling of empowerment to deliver a good presentation.

How do you feel now as someone who gives speeches for a living or as part of your job? Describe what goes through your head and what do you feel like when you get a speaking gig, once you're preparing, the day of the speech, and once you start speaking.

Some things never change -- my students are stunned when I tell them that I still get nervous, after all these years. But I subscribe to the theory that a speaker has to "earn the right to be confident." In other words, when I take on a new class, or a new speaking gig, sure, I'm nervous. I should be, since I have no idea what I am going to do or say. But as the lecture notes/speaking notes start to take shape, the confidence grows and the "dread" turns into eagerness – the adrenaline rush is still there, but it shifts from negative to positive energy.

How did you make progress from the time you were a student to now? What did you do to improve as a speaker?

I spoke in a variety of venues, from contests to earn scholarship money to intercollegiate speech and debate competitions to citizen venues. After each speech, I try to evaluate what I did well (the stuff I can do again) and what didn't go well – what I still need to work on. I don't aim for a "perfect speech," as that doesn't exist. But each one can be better than the last.

What did you do to increase your confidence?

Prepare and practice! I am always amazed at my students that are writing out their speaking note cards in class right before giving a speech, and then they wonder why they are so nervous -- It's because you haven't practiced, even *once*, to see how you will actually deliver this speech! Five, six, or seven complete rehearsals, using the finished speaking notes, builds the confidence you'll need. Right before getting up in front of the audience, I still employ deep breathing methods to take that final edge off at the beginning of the speech.

What do you do to stay in the moment and enjoy your time presenting in front of a crowd?

Using direct eye contact during the presentation, to just one person at a time, reinforces that people are understanding and enjoying the message you are presenting. It creates a bond with the audience, but on a one-to-one basis; it also takes away some of the nervousness of "oh-my-god-everybody-is-looking-at-me" and replaces it with individual conversations with individual audience members.

What positive thoughts go through your mind as you're presenting these days?

"This is working."
"They are getting my message."
"People are listening, paying attention."
"This is information that will empower these folks."

What tips would you give to new speakers? Does it get easier? How did it get easier for you?

Treat public speaking like you would any other performance with spectators, from music to sports. If you are a singer or musician, and you are asked to play or sing a song for a performance, how much practice would you put in? Before a big game, how much practice does a good team put in? If a player decided they didn't need to practice, what would the coach say? The nervousness never goes away completely, and it shouldn't. But it gets easier with practice and experience.

What last piece of advice would you impart to new speakers?

Trust yourself. The more "crutches" you build into your speech, the more you hinder your growth. Thousands of people do this every day that are not nearly as smart and talented as you are.

Remember, you didn't successfully ride a bike the first time you tried. But when you fell down and skinned your knee, you didn't put the training wheels back on – you tried and failed again and again. But once you were able to really ride that bike, and realized "I can do this," that sense of freedom and accomplishment was amazing.

<u>Resources</u>

Answers to Common Public Speaking Questions

Q: How do I eliminate "ums" "likes" and other nonfluencies/paralanguage when I give a speech (or filler words)?

A: I had a huge issue with using way too many "likes" in daily conversations until I became a Teaching Assistant.

My first group of college students (who were practically my age) would give me a hard time about it occasionally, all in good fun. However, I started realizing I needed to really do something about it if I was going to be seen as a professional speaker (and even more so when I was asked to teach a Voice and Articulation class one semester).

I started listening to books on tape constantly, thinking more about what I was saying, and putting on more of a "professional face" and professional speaking voice when I went into the classroom, so I didn't fall into the "like" trap.

I do have to say, I think becoming more confident with the content I was speaking about was also key. For new speakers, that would translate to "practice your material until you do not need to use filler words in place of your actual speech content."

Listening to books on tape was enormously helpful as a passive way to fix the problem. I've been listening to them for years now, every time I get in the car, and I am so much more comfortable with my presentations.

Q: What do I do with my hands while I present?

A: Some people instinctively know what to do with their hands while they are presenting, but it's a little harder for some people.

I suggest watching the helpful video "Make Body Language Your Superpower by Stanford School of Business" and the "What Do I

Do With My Hands" video that are both recommended in this section. They have some very distinct suggestions.

I would also recommend presenting your speech in a seated position with an audience, before you attempt it standing up, if you are having trouble with gestures. Many people naturally gesture when they are having a conversation with someone while seated. Then stand up and try to maintain the same gesturing style

Q: I'm afraid I might start pacing or fidgeting during my speech. What type of purposeful movements should I use?

A: It depends on what type of speech you're giving. I normally tell my beginner students that they can stay planted in one spot throughout the entire speech, as long as they use dynamic and purposeful hand gestures, and stand near the audience (some people try to hide behind the podium or glue themselves to the wall).

I also tell them that if they are giving the typical 5-7 minute student speech, they can walk the length of the room once or twice during that time period, at a casual pace, as long as they keep their body angled toward the audience and don't lose that connection with the audience.

If you are a paid speaker, you'll need to do some moving around, whether it's subtle or more dynamic (unless you are being paid to give a traditional manuscript speech, in which case you will most likely stay behind the lectern).

As a paid speaker, hired for delivering a valuable message and engaging an audience, you will need to consider what type of audience will be there, think about the type of speech you are presenting, and what type of stage or area you will be presenting on.

Watch some Google videos that you assume will be similar to your own speaking situation, and see what kind of movements those speakers use. You can mimic those as you practice, until you have made it feel like your own.

Q: How can I feel more comfortable establishing eye contact?

A: Whatever you do, don't stare above the heads of your audience members, or at their ears or foreheads. Some people think this is a great trick when giving a speech. If you are in an auditorium with hundreds of speakers, you might be able to get away with it, but most audiences will know you are not looking at them.

You will feel more comfortable making eye contact if you have made an effort to chat with some of your audience members before starting your presentation. In that case, it will feel like an extension of the conversation you had with them previously, just as if you were talking with friends at dinner.

I normally tell my student speakers to find 3 friendly faces to the left, center, and right of the audience, so they don't end up favoring one particular spot. You can also place your friends strategically throughout the audience so you will have familiar faces to make eye contact with (If your friends are in attendance, tell them to also smile at you endlessly, so you'll remember to smile on stage!).

Q: What if I'm not loud enough?

A: I tell my soft-spoken students to practice being overly and perhaps obnoxiously loud. That way on speech day, they actually talk at the perfect volume.

Q: I can never stay within a given time limit. It's not really required, though, right?

A: So many people feel like a time limit is really just a suggestion, but this a huge misconception. In speech classes, teachers emphasize staying within the time limit, not just for the sake of keeping the student speeches and course schedule on track, but also to prepare students for future speeches outside the classroom.

Most events where you might be invited or paid to speak also have a schedule, and if you are one of the main speakers, you will most likely be asked to speak for 45-60 minutes. If you run significantly under or over the time limit, you will end up looking very unprofessional and may have a hard time finding future invitations. You should know your material well enough, and have practiced enough times, that you have a good idea of how long you'll take.

Q: Why can't public speaking be just like a conversation with my friends? Why is it so different and terrifying?

A: Ready for a quick history lesson? Humans are biologically designed to get an adrenaline-rush to prepare them for demanding physical tasks, like running away from a dangerous animal or hunting for survival. We're also scared to speak in front of large groups because many centuries ago, there was a very logical fear of not being accepted by the "tribe." If you were shunned for some unfavorable act, that meant that you would be left on your own, likely to die without the protection of the group.

For a quick explanation of our biology and how you can use it to help you, see this insightful article from Forbes.com:

Why We Fear Public Speaking and How To Overcome It
http://www.forbes.com/sites/nickmorgan/2011/03/30/why-we-fear-public-speaking-and-how-to-overcome-it/3/

For a really long (but incredibly entertaining) explanation of our biology and why/how it impacts our desire to fit in, see this helpful article:

Taming the Mammoth: Why You Should Stop Caring What Other People Think
http://waitbutwhy.com/2014/06/taming-mammoth-let-peoples-opinions-run-life.html

Q: How can I connect with my audience more? I talk to customers so much that I feel like I've just become too direct, impolite, or detached.

A: I get this question frequently in my online speech classes and it always catches me off guard. Remember that your speech is not for you, if you are really understanding and learning the important aspects of public speaking, you will appreciate the fact that you have designed this message just for your audience.

Treat them how you would like to be treated, and continue winning them over every minute of your speech. You can do this by talking about things they can relate to, using some personal examples, maintaining good volume, vocal inflection, a conversational tone, thorough eye contact, smiling, and using words like "you" and "we" throughout your speech to establish a connection.

Q: Is it okay to memorize my speech word for word?

A: This is a tricky question. It depends. If you're taking a speech class in high school or college, you will be asked to prepare and present mostly extemporaneous speeches.

That means you will be very familiar with what you want to say every step of the way (through practicing using the 9 steps in Step 1 of this book), but it will not be memorized, so it might change slightly with each presentation. You will also have some speaking notes (i.e. note cards) with key phrases written on them to help guide you just a bit through your speech. People giving speeches at weddings normally speak extemporaneously.

If you are memorizing something for a play or drama class, please memorize it! Otherwise, your instructor might send me an angry email.

If you are paid to present a speech at an event or you are a keynote speaker, what you will be doing is much more like acting, and you will be paid a pretty good fee. So yes, memorize your presentation word for word (but never let it *sound* memorized) and practice it word for word as many times as humanly possible to maintain your good reputation.

Q: How can I avoid rambling?

A: I have found that most speakers either ramble at the very beginning of their speech (they're just not sure how to get started) or at the very end of their speech (they're just not sure how to conclude).

The best way to avoid this is to know, word for word, what your opening statements will be, and what your closing statements will be. Resist the urge to mutter and mumble nonsensical words in these spots (I see it all the time).

Have your opening and closing at the forefront of your mind, so that when you feel yourself about to let your message spin out of control, you can grab those lines, deliver them, and either proceed, or pause and wait for applause before you sit back down (I promise they will figure out that you've finished, just wait patiently for applause, stay strong, and whatever you do, do not end your speech with "That's it.").

If you tend to ramble throughout your speech, this is because your speech is probably not completely ready. Be sure you are prepared for an extemporaneous speech, know where you are headed in your speech, and be sure you have practiced numerous times.

Q: I feel like I could talk all day long and never get to my point. How can I clearly and directly get my point across?

A: First, have a clear purpose and thesis statement as soon as you begin preparing your speech content. It is very easy to veer all over the place when you prepare and present a speech if you never established where you were headed in the first place.

If you have a clear thesis statement, every time you feel yourself making progress in your organization and research, take a quick look at your thesis to be sure you haven't veered off into new territory. Little checks like this throughout your preparation will help.

However, if you trick yourself into thinking your thesis is clear and it's not, you are going to have a very hard time as you prepare and present (I have seen it many times, including this week).

Now if you're thinking, "Yeah, I do that while I'm preparing, but I still go off on tangents and never get my point across when I'm *presenting*," then you need to practice out loud a lot more than you might be used to.

You are probably getting off track because different ideas get triggered while you're speaking, and you decide to just go with it (this can also lead to rambling). Avoid that temptation! You know what the main ideas and supporting ideas should be in your speech, so stick closely to your material for the sake of your audience, your time, and your message.

Q: I'm so nervous in front of big crowds. What do I do?

A: Take a look at Step 2 of this book, and use those tips to build up your confidence. The best piece of advice I can give you is to practice in front of small groups of people, repeatedly, and gradually increase to larger groups of people.

If you have done this repeatedly, then by the time you have to speak in front of that big crowd, it's nothing new. The crowd size is familiar, how you feel in regards to your anxiety will be familiar, and your content will be familiar. It will be nothing you haven't handled before.

Q: How can I get from one main point to the next in a way that makes sense and doesn't sound choppy?

A: You can use signposts ("Next," "Moving on," "To conclude," etc.) or more thorough transitional statements. Both are easy, clear, and get the job done.

My students typically do not like using transitional statements that are overtly obvious between main points (which I require) like, "Now that we have talked about main point one: oranges, let's move on to our next point: bananas." However, you don't have to use such tired and overused phrasing. You are welcome to get more creative. You could say something like, "Now that we have talked about one of the more popular citrus fruits, let's move on to everyone's favorite breakfast fruit, bananas."

If you are in a speech class, your teacher will most likely expect you to use some sort of transitional statement between main points, and eventually you will probably find them to be more helpful than you expected (I even use them in lecture; it's a great way to remind your audience what you have been talking about and help them tune back in).

However, if you are speaking for work or an event, there may be different ways you're expected to move from point to point in your speech. If all else fails and you're at a loss, definitely go with some clear-cut transitions.

Q: How can I get over this once and for all? I feel like I'm asked to give a speech once every few years, just frequently enough that it terrifies me, but not frequently enough that I get used to it.

A: Here's the answer everyone loves to hear (just kidding): Join Toastmasters! I will admit, I'm not a member, but it doesn't mean I haven't looked into joining.

You can join other organizations where you will get the opportunity to speak, but if you feel you still might find yourself avoiding speaking situations within those organizations, Toastmasters is the way to go. You'll be with a friendly group of people in the same situation as you, who want to challenge themselves and continue to become better speakers.

The key is to continue doing things outside your comfort zone, and the more often, the better.

Public speaking is less like riding a bike and more like working out (unfortunately). You simply can't stay away from speaking opportunities for a few years and expect to feel just as confident as you did previously. In other words, it's not as easy as getting back on the bike. You will have to build those public speaking muscles again until you are strong and confident.

~

For more information about Toastmasters, check out this helpful blog post from the website Speaking About Presenting (which is also fantastic):

How to get the most out of Toastmasters
http://www.speakingaboutpresenting.com/presentation-philosophy/how-to-get-the-most-out-of-toastmasters/

Tips for Using Technology in Your Presentation

Many people reading this book are likely online speech students. I wrote a large portion of this content with them in mind, since nearly all of them suffer from a more intense fear of public speaking than other students (hence, taking the class online instead of face-to-face).

It's nothing to be ashamed of. It is only natural that an online option might initially appear to free you of all your public speaking worries, but I'm afraid that's not necessarily true. There will also be additional components you'll need to concern yourself with.

The problem with online presentations is that many people think they can take a course online, have job interviews via Skype in the comfort of their own home, or attend a webinar for work without having to put in the same amount of effort or without the same feeling of anxiety.

Not exactly.

As someone who has taught online speech classes for a number of years, held webinars for my online classes, participated in webinars for work, had job interviews over the phone, and listened to the details of my colleagues' job interviews via Skype, I've learned a thing or two about this new public speaking arena.

Some of the findings might surprise you.

Below are some interviews with online public speaking instructors who have webinar and online presentation experience themselves. If you happen to be an online student or someone who may have to be part of a webcam meeting for work, the following may be helpful.

<u>Erin Lovell Ebanks</u>
<u>Public Speaking instructor for online and face-to-face classes</u>

How can students prepare for an online speech? Specifically, what things should they do to practice their delivery?

Prepare the same way you would for an actual speech in class. If you don't take it as seriously, you will likely end up putting much more time and effort into take after take of your speech because of lack of preparation. I have received frustrated emails from numerous students about this in the past. You can't expect to set up a camera and miraculously know exactly how to present a speech you haven't prepared for.

Depending on the school where you are doing your online speech course, though, you may need an audience of 5 people, or you may not actually need an audience. Regardless, students report getting nervous to record a professional speech in front of the camera, knowing that their professor and fellow classmates will be evaluating them, so you need plenty of rehearsals.

If a person isn't skilled in technology, can they successfully take an online speaking course and/or attend virtual conferences/webinar meetings in which they might need to present? What kind of technological skills and delivery skills should they focus on?

You do not have to be technologically savvy to take online courses or attend a virtual conference. However, it would be a great idea to watch some tutorials online to learn how to use the different systems the school or company will be using. If they are not clear about what learning management system (i.e. Blackboard, Canvas, Sakai, etc.) or webinar service (Adobe Connect, GoToMeeting, etc.) they'll be using, email one of the leaders directly, so you can learn aspects of the technology ahead of time.

Many systems do not require advanced knowledge of any kind, but you need to be aware of what you'll be using, and some basics to get you through the class or meeting. You will also need to understand that the work and preparation you put into your webcam presentation will be the same as if all of it was happening face-to-face. Be careful not to deceive yourself into putting in less effort; it's one of the biggest mistakes I have seen as a facilitator.

One of the biggest problems I see with online students is that they sit down during their speech, don't look at the camera, cut their head out of view (or only record their head rather than the rest of their body), record themselves from an odd angle, or stay immersed in the shadows. This is all so new for them! Where should they stand? Where should they look? How should they carry themselves so they look confident and professional? What do you think are the most important things to remember when delivering a presentation for an online audience?

A few good guidelines for online speech classes are:
- Film yourself from the knees up so your instructor can fully evaluate your posture and gestures. Do not sit down.
- Film a short clip of yourself first, and check it to see if the camera is positioned properly before you start filming the speech in its entirety.
- Dress professionally. It shows that you are taking the assignment seriously and it will impress your instructor. This will also most likely help you carry yourself more professionally and confidently.
- If you have an audience present while the camera rolls, make eye contact with them. If it's just you and the camera, you can just make eye contact with the camera.

A few good guidelines for virtual conferences/webinar meetings:
- Unlike online speeches, you will be sitting down as you attend or present.
- Frame your head and the tops of your shoulders in the webcam (test this out ahead of time). If you are too far back, or too close, it might make others feel uncomfortable.

- Dress professionally for the meeting, and sit up straight to convey your professionalism and confidence.
- Prepare whatever materials are necessary ahead of time.

The most important thing to remember is that you still need to "get into character" in these situations. I have tried attending webinar meetings after having just cooked a meal, or some other completely unrelated activity, but I find that I have to give myself time to get into the proper mindset. Otherwise, the contrast throws me off a bit, and I don't present my best self.

What other advice do you have for students who now have to present online for school and job opportunities (i.e. an online speech class, Skype interview for a job, or Web conference)?

To reiterate everything else I have said above, prepare and practice. Treat it as if it was happening in person, face-to-face. I'll be honest, one time during grad school, I had a telephone interview that was a first for me (it wasn't online, but I believe it's applicable here). I felt more casual going into it, which meant I seemed under-prepared. I could tell that was how I came off, and I never got a final interview. It helped me to learn the important lesson of treating the situation formally. So last year when I had another telephone interview, I spoke, dressed, and stood confidently and professionally, even though no one could see me. I believe it helped me get into character more, and the professionalism was conveyed. To this day I dress professionally when I attend or hold webinars from home, even if the meeting is audio only.

Public Speaking instructor for online and face-to-face classes

Q: How can students prepare for an online speech? Specifically, what things should they do to practice their delivery?

A: I encourage students to practice at least 5 to 6 times; if they can record their rehearsals and re-watch themselves, even better. Practice is crucial and viewing yourself presenting a speech is usually a pleasant surprise, as most are performing much better than they think they are, and can easily correct mistakes.

Q: If a person isn't skilled in technology, can they successfully take an online speaking course and/or attend virtual conferences/webinar meetings in which they'll need to present? What kind of technological skills and delivery skills should they focus on?

A: Students do need basic technology skills to participate in any online course. In an online speech course, there are several additional skills which are required. A student must know (at least, in some schools) how to use a camera and record using YouTube. There are several settings that must be configured properly. A student must also have the skill to upload a video into the course following the required instructions. Generally, these skills are relatively simple to acquire, but can be quite anxiety-provoking on the first attempts.

Q: One of the biggest problems I see with online students is that they sit down during their speech, don't look at the camera, cut their head out of view (or only record their head rather than the rest of their body), record themselves from an odd angle, or stay immersed in the shadows. This is all so new for them! Where should they stand? Where should they look? How should they carry themselves so they look confident and professional? What do you think are the most important things

to remember when delivering a presentation for an online audience?

A: A student should select an area in their home or workplace with as little clutter and visual distractions as possible. Present yourself professionally! Know that giving a speech is a special day, and students should present themselves in such a way that they are attempting to create a good impression with their audience. Dress up. Present yourself in a way that you might for a job interview. Maintain eye contact with your audience, and be conversational in your delivery. In other words, use vocal variety, speak clearly, (avoid filler words such as "um" and "like") smile, and stand up straight.

Q: What other advice do you have for students who now have to visually present themselves online for school and job opportunities (i.e. an online speech class, Skype interview for a job, or Web conference)?

A: As with most things in life, as we gain more experience we improve. If this is only your first or second speech class, remember your speech or presentation does not have to be perfect. Just be prepared, know your content, show interest in the material you are presenting, and practice as much as possible.

Public Speaking instructor for online and face-to-face classes

Q: How can students prepare for an online speech? Specifically, what things should they do to practice their delivery?

A: Don't procrastinate! It's important to start writing your speech early and get feedback from your instructor to make sure you're on track. When practicing your delivery, make sure you practice aloud and look in a mirror or video record yourself to see your delivery. Then practice in front of family and friends and get their feedback. Practice your eye contact and vary your voice for the vocal delivery.

Q: If a person isn't skilled in technology, can they successfully take an online speaking course and/or attend virtual conferences/webinar meetings in which they'll need to present? What kind of technological skills and delivery skills should they focus on?

A: Yes! Absolutely, just make sure that you stay on top of your deadlines and ask whenever you need help in an online class. You should click on every link, giving yourself a "tour" of the class. For a webinar or conference on Google Hangout or Skype, you should also practice with an online friend so that you get used to presenting in front of the computer screen.

Q: One of the biggest problems I see with online students is that they sit down during their speech, don't look at the camera, cut their head out of view (or only record their head rather than the rest of their body), record themselves from an odd angle, or stay immersed in the shadows. This is all so new for them! Where should they stand? Where should they look? How should they carry themselves so they look confident and professional? What do you think are the most important things to remember when delivering a presentation for an online audience?

A: They get too comfortable and they sit down during a speech-
I've seen it many times! Make sure you're standing and dressed in
business casual attire; it can make you feel more confident in your
speech. For the recording, do a small test run. Say a few sentences
while taping and then watch yourself. Make sure that we can see
you clearly and hear you clearly. Be sure you know your speech
well enough that you can present with confidence and really show
us you know what you're talking about!

**Q: What other advice do you have for students who now have
to visually present themselves online for school and job
opportunities (i.e. an online speech class, Skype interview for a
job, or Web conference)?**

A: I recently shot a web interview, where the program video
recorded my answers. I have never done an interview in that
format and it was really interesting. So make sure you take
advantage of the practice questions. I was able to answer practice
questions that videotaped me and I could see myself give my
answers. Look straight into the camera as if you are talking to a
person and speak in a conversational manner.

Assistant Director of Communication Arts Online at a Florida university

Q: How can students prepare for an online speech? Specifically, what things should they do to practice their delivery?

A: As with everything in life, practice is the essential piece of the puzzle that brings everything together. One should practice just enough that they begin to feel comfortable, but not so much that it sounds like they're reading from a book. The speaker needs to be professional, yet conversational.

Q: If a person isn't skilled in technology, can they successfully take an online speaking course and/or attend virtual conferences/webinar meetings in which they'll need to present? What kind of technological skills and delivery skills should they focus on?

A: In the world today, technology is everywhere. If you are unsure of how to do something, you can just type it into Google and instantly 20 different solutions come up. The advice that I can provide to students is to have a strong Internet connection, and to test the site/virtual conference room prior to entering for real. The test should include that the video camera works, the microphone is on (and not too loud), and that your audience can hear you. Be sure you have all this properly set up a few minutes before you start.

Q: One of the biggest problems I see with online students is that they sit down during their speech, don't look at the camera, cut their head out of view (or only record their head rather than the rest of their body), record themselves from an odd angle, or stay immersed in the shadows. This is all so new for them! Where should they stand? Where should they look? How should they carry themselves so they look confident and professional? What do you think are the most important things to remember when delivering a presentation for an online audience?

A: This may be one of the more common items that come up for student speeches. My advice here is to see if your university offers a conference room that you can rent with a podium, and either rent or borrow an HD camera to use (the university IT department may let you rent one out). This way you can essentially mimic a real atmosphere to give the speech in. It is difficult to use your room or kitchen as a place to give a speech (not to mention using visual aids), therefore using a conference room or classroom would be ideal.

Q: What other advice do you have for students who now have to visually present themselves online for school and job opportunities (i.e. an online speech class, Skype interview for a job, or Web conference)?

A: One other piece of advice that I would give to students is to take this part seriously. Just because the speech, interview or conference is online does not mean that you should treat it any differently than a face-to-face situation. This includes being professional, dressing to impress (business professional recommended, with business casual being a must), and coming off as it you've prepared, just as if you were meeting/presenting in person.

Advice for Those with High Communication Apprehension

There might be some of you out there who, after reading this book, still feel discouraged.

You might be one of the rare individuals who suffer from extremely high communication apprehension (fear of communicating with others) either due to environmental factors (i.e. the culture and/or environment you were raised in), genetic traits, personality traits, or a combination of a number of factors.

I promise there is a way to get through it.

Interview

Bio:

Shari Hodgson is a full-time faculty member and in 2012 took on an administrative position as the General Education Program Scheduler and Assessment Coordinator in the Nicholson School at the University of Central Florida.

In addition to her full-time faculty position, Ms. Hodgson has worked in the private sector as a consultant in a myriad of different communication trainings and seminars. Their focus included intra-interpersonal relationships in business, teambuilding, and for twenty-two years helping to improve the communication outcomes and lowering the recidivism rates of federal inmates. She also worked in Trial communications offering continuing legal education to attorneys. Her efforts to improve communication systems in incorporate and community organizations were just acknowledged by the Winter Park Chamber of Commerce by awarding her the first "Lifetime Achievement Award" for her twenty-five years of service.

EE: How long have you been presenting or performing as part of your job?

SH: I have been presenting all my life, and I've been fearful of presenting all my life. However, it was during my middle and high school years when I was an officer in student government, and I was forced to campaign and speak to assemblies of 300 student meetings that my terror began to paralyze me. It necessitated that I incorporate anxiety-reducing strategies: deep breathing, positive self-talk, and visualizations.

EE: In terms of today, how often do you present before a crowd?

SH: I present every day! And with all the different types of training and consulting work performed, I present to 25 to 300 audience members.

EE: So how did you feel as a high school or college student giving speeches in class? I want to know what went through your head. I think this will be so valuable to new speakers.

SH: When I was about six-years-old, in an effort to help me think, my father would quiz us on different math problems, questions about history or current events to check our knowledge.

In order to please him, I would answer anything. Mind you, this started when I was six-years-old and often times, I would get the answer wrong.

My older sister would then give the correct answer. He would praise her, criticize me, and I felt very, very stupid. What that led to was that every time I got asked a question later in school I would feel panicky. That still happens to me today, during committee meetings or any situation where the leader or authority figure is asking an unfamiliar question, I still feel anxious and apprehensive about giving my answer.

That fear has never gone away. So, naturally even in class, when I'm teaching and a student is being rather challenging, I have to slow myself down and breathe.

My fear of making a mistake happened in my home. My internal critical voice would kick in immediately, and warn me to watch what I say and don't make a mistake.

EE: Did you have to give speeches in high school, and can you recall how you felt?

SH: Oh, yes. I had to give speeches. I remember getting called on to get up to do a math problem on the blackboard and I just froze. I couldn't even get out of my desk. I remember that first grade teacher being mad at me. It came from my fear of doing it wrong.

I always had to overcome that belief system that I was stupid. I did have a learning disability. Of course, that diagnosis didn't exist when I was in school. They didn't know anything about learning disabilities.

EE: How did you overcome this? How did you make progress from then until now? Or maybe it was really tiny steps which led to bigger steps?

SH: Here's the interesting thing. I don't know whether this is going to make sense. I always found myself in positions of leadership. I believe now looking back, it was divine providence. But for me, it just seemed that I ended up in positions of leadership and having to give speeches.

All of a sudden, I'd be in the hot seat and in a position where I had to perform in front of people and I had to say to myself, it just felt like, "Okay Shari, here it is." You just have to overcome your fear and do it.

EE: Your confidence or being in those leadership roles, did that help you to build your confidence?

SH: Absolutely. Now remember, I felt the fear. And I did it anyway. That has been my motto since I was probably twelve-years-old, "feel the fear and do it anyway."

EE: Were there any other specific things you would do? Like deep breaths, or positive self-talk that helped you to get better?

SH: I don't know that I did that consciously until I got into high school. And then, yes, in high school, I would definitely use positive self-talk.

Deep Breathing also helped. But I learned this technique as a child. I had very severe asthma. My mother would work with me in terms of doing what I learned later was self-hypnosis. She would lay me on the bed when I would get into these attacks where I couldn't breath, and she would say, "Now I want you to breathe in the good and blow out the bad. Breathe in the good. Blow out the bad."

And, she would give me imaginary colors of the air that I was breathing. So, from childhood I began practicing what science has now affirmed as coping strategies for communication apprehension. I wrote an article regarding these techniques for the textbook *Between One and Many*; the Brydon and Scott book.

EE: So these days, what do you do to stay in the moment and enjoy your time presenting in front of a crowd?

SH: I think what has happened to me is that I have learned to care more about my audience, and what they are learning, than my performance.

This way of framing a rhetorical situation started when I began teaching speech twenty-five years ago. I just fell in love with my students. I was so committed to their success, that if I had to stand on my head or make a fool of myself, I'd do whatever it took for my students to become comfortable and passionate about becoming effective speakers.

EE: That seems to be a common thread in these interviews. What positive thoughts go through your mind as you present?

SH: My positive thoughts seem to be a result of my connection and my commitment to students. As I'm lecturing, if I see a student smile or nod their head, that's what calms me down. That's what gives me my sense that, "Okay, I'm getting through to my students and this is my goal."

It is also important to remember the current attention span is about 14 minutes; it's important to continually engage students in some form of discussion about what we just covered to ensure they are awake and learning.

EE: So that helps. Keeping that connection?

SH: One of the things that I started when I was starting my consulting business and having to do presentations, is that I would usually start my presentation by asking the audience to demonstrate something or I'd ask them a question of relevance to their lives. This was a great way to make them feel important and to ensure audience engagement. And, an important personal benefit is that it also gives me time to calm down during the first three minutes of being in front of an audience by removing the pressure to perform.

EE: Yes. It establishes an immediate bond.

SH: Then, when I did communication foundation research, I discovered that audience engagement during the first minute or two of your speech is effective to increase audience listening and thus learning.

EE: What tips would you give to new speakers? Does it get easier and how did it get easier for you? What tips would you give them?

SH: I think my most important tip would be for them to find a way, personally, to become an other-centered speaker versus a self-centered speaker.

EE: That's great. What last piece of advice would you impart to new students?

SH: To love the process of becoming an excellent speaker. Because it's going to last you all of your life. That your work never ends. It's a personal process of evolving and this process is endless.

Every time I teach, every time I consult, every time I present, every time I experience public speaking, I am becoming a better communicator.

My favorite question to ask new students is, "Is knowledge power?" Of course their first response is "YES!" I then remind them, "Not until your knowledge is communicated effectively."

Books

7 Steps to Fearless Speaking by Lilyan Wilder

High Impact Communication: How to Build Charisma, Credibility, and Trust by Bert Decker

Stage Fright: 40 Stars Tell You How They Beat America's #1 Fear by Mick Berry, MFA and Michael R. Edelstein, PhD.

Stage Fright: A Student-Friendly Guide to Managing the Jitters by George Griffin

Talk Like TED: The 9 Public-Speaking Secrets of the World's Top Minds by Carmine Gallo

The Essentials of Public Speaking for Technical Presentations by Cheryl Hamilton et al.

The Naked Presenter: Delivering Powerful Presentations With or Without Slides by Garr Reynolds

Recommended Videos

Videos I have created for my speech students (feel free to use them as you see fit!)

(For fast access, go to the Erin Lovell Ebanks YouTube channel to find all of my speech tip videos and short lecture videos I've listed throughout this Resources section, or use the following link: https://www.youtube.com/channel/UCPRF9bYsuWs0NXCUe2kz6p Q)

The videos are listed in the order they should be watched for new speakers and students

3 Basics to Give a Great Speech
https://www.youtube.com/watch?v=Z6ZxLC0PAFA

The Secret to Overcoming Public Speaking Nerves
https://www.youtube.com/watch?v=p_DuRGPfR8s

Introduction Speech Guidelines
https://www.youtube.com/watch?v=velb6Dt85Ww

Group Presentation Guidelines
https://www.youtube.com/watch?v=yRDOTq7wLnA

Informative Speech Guidelines
https://www.youtube.com/watch?v=7buGxIrWgH8

Persuasive Speech Guidelines
https://www.youtube.com/watch?v=9EQ8Ph22lBw

Videos for the communication classroom and public speaking workshops

Amy Cuddy: Your Body Language Shapes Who You Are (TED Talk)
https://www.youtube.com/watch?v=Ks-_Mh1QhMc

Don McMillan: Life After Death by PowerPoint
https://www.youtube.com/watch?v=KbSPPFYxx3o

Dr. Ivan Joseph: The Skill of Self Confidence (TEDxRyersonU)
https://www.youtube.com/watch?v=w-HYZv6HzAs

How to Be a Great Public Speaker: Patricia Fripp at Toastmasters International
https://www.youtube.com/watch?v=24203BR_axc

Kelli McGonical: How to Make Stress Your Friend (TED Talk)
https://www.youtube.com/watch?v=RcGyVTAoXEU

Lars Sudmann: On Public Speaking (TEDxFlanders)
https://www.youtube.com/watch?v=AdRuBRR6xOU

Make Body Language Your Superpower by Stanford School of Business
https://www.youtube.com/watch?v=cFLjudWTuGQ

Nancy Duarte: The Secret Structure of Great Talks (TEDxEast)
https://www.youtube.com/watch?v=1nYFpuc2Umk

Ep 5. What Do I Do With My Hands - Presentation Skills - Public Speaking
https://www.youtube.com/watch?v=STkFEYPmb14

(Andrew Bryant from Self Leadership International, has quite a few episodes in the BananaMana TV YouTube Channel that include excellent tips for new public speakers, that also answer some important presentation questions.)

Notes & Activities for Use in the Classroom/Workshops

If you are a speech instructor who would like to use *The 3-Step Speech* in the classroom, or a presenter who would like to use it for workshops, I suggest creating short and insightful quizzes based on the brief videos and activities below. Before I quiz students, we normally discuss the following ideas in more detail, or I will assign them to watch the short YouTube or lecture videos I have provided throughout this Resources section. I encourage you to have discussions with your audience members/students about why they chose the answers they did.

The following notes are loosely based on the following textbooks I use in my own classrooms:

Between One and Many: The Art & Science of Public Speaking by Brydon and Scott

DK Guide to Public Speaking (2nd Edition) by Lisa A. Ford-Brown

Public Speaking: An Audience-Centered Approach (9th Edition) by Beebe and Beebe

Public Speaking Handbook (4th Edition) by Beebe and Beebe

The Essentials of Public Speaking for Technical Presentations by Cheryl Hamilton et al.

~
-How public speaking benefits you-

Helps you:
Learn how to analyze an audience
Adapt ideas to specific audiences
Advance in your career

-Important steps in planning and preparing a speech-

1. Analyze your audience
*Respect the diversity of your audience- Be careful not to offend anyone
*Organize your message carefully: Intro, Body, Conclusion
*Use the best language for your audience- Acronyms and jargon are not as effective as simple, more conversational language
*Be energetic, also be yourself

2. Develop your topic, purpose, thesis, and key ideas
*In planning your speech topic, determine:
Purpose- What is the point of your speech, why are you giving it (What type of speech is it: Informative, Persuasive, Special Occasion, etc.)
Pick something you are familiar with, interested in, that your audience will be interested in, and that fits the requirements for the assignment.

*In planning your speech organization:
Plan your thesis statement
Decide on and develop some key ideas that you can narrow down to 2-5 main points

3: Outline your speech
*Have an attention-getting hook and introduction (thesis followed by your preview), then construct the body of your speech with 2-5 main points. Finally, finish by restating your 3 main points or summarizing in a meaningful way, and include a wrap-up statement.

Audience/classroom participation: Have the class pick a few ideas from a list of sample speech topics. You can write them up on the board, then have the class help you narrow down the list to one speech topic based on the above-listed four requirements. At this point you can have the class can help you work on an outline on the board.

Watch this helpful video for more tips:

YouTube: How to Pick a Public Speech Topic: Tips for Interesting Speech Topics
https://www.youtube.com/watch?v=EkpUp2Gn19w

4: Rehearse
*Rehearse your speech out loud (not in your head), and use your visual aids when you practice.

-Ethics-

Research your content thoroughly and be careful not to plagiarize
Watch this video for some helpful tips:
YouTube: How to do Research for a Speech
https://www.youtube.com/watch?v=T7ekc7MehL4

Conduct personal interviews: Decide who to interview, contact them, prepare your questions, be polite during the interview, take notes, and be sure to record them. Review and expand your interview notes afterward, and send them a thank you card!

Audience/classroom participation idea: Ask two audience members to come up to the front and act as if one is being interviewed and the other is the interviewee to demonstrate how to properly (and/or improperly) interview someone.

-Be aware of audience feedback-

Visual (facial expressions), vocal (laughter), and verbal (comment) are all types of feedback your audience might be giving to you as you present. Adjust your speech accordingly if you do not feel your audience is engaged or interested.

-To be most effective as a persuasive speaker, use Aristotle's Persuasive Appeals-

<u>Logos</u> (appeal to logic)- Your audience is persuaded by your message because it makes logical sense (ex. you were organized & presented evidence)

<u>Pathos</u> (appeal to emotion)- Your audience is persuaded by your message because it makes you feel something (ex. your provided emotional stories)

<u>Ethos</u> (appeal to the audience's perception of the speaker's credibility)- Your audience is persuaded by your message they feel you are an ethical and trustworthy person (ex. you cited your sources)

-Plan your speech so it appeals to your particular audience-

Know who your listeners are. Be aware of the situational, demographic, and psychological information about your audience to communicate with them most effectively.

-Supporting materials to look for as you research-

Find interesting pictures and graphs to make your speech more engaging and clarify and confusing information.

Audience/classroom participation idea: Show the class how Google images can help you with this, and show them a clip of a TED video that used effective supporting materials.

-Use an attention-getter-

Hook your audience by using a quote, shocking statistic, question, demonstration, etc. as a way to open with impact.

Audience/classroom participation idea: The presenter and/or an audience member can present various attention-getters and have the audience guess which is which.

<u>Motivate your audience</u>: Give your audience a reason to listen to your speech during or immediately after you have opened with impact. Maybe you will be motivating them by stating that your speech will help them learn something new, save time, earn money, or gain the skills to be healthier.

<u>Be credible</u>: Be sure to present yourself and your information in a way that will make the audience respect you and like you.

Audience/classroom participation idea: What are some ways you might do this in an upcoming speech?

Audience/classroom participation idea: Watch the following video to have a few laughs with your audience, and discuss afterward how the speaker did *not* establish credibility and likeability with the audience. What are some ways he could have been a more credible speaker?

Big Bang Theory- Sheldon's Speech
https://www.youtube.com/watch?v=hAElfmG2H2Y

-Open and end with impact-

Primacy and recency effect: Be sure that the beginning and end of your speech have impact, they are the parts people tend to remember.

Audience/classroom participation idea: Watch the following videos with your students to discuss what openings and closings everyone liked best? In what way was the opening or closing effective?

How to start your speech (3 excellent openings)
https://www.youtube.com/watch?v=tCBZQ8Jvg9k

How to end your speech (3 excellent closings)
https://www.youtube.com/watch?v=R3wlW6PaTsA

Final audience/classroom participation idea: After your students have learned the basics of developing a speech, pass out a word search with 10 words to find (you can find easy-to-use word search generators online). Give them 2 minutes and reward the person who finds the most speech terms. Then ask volunteers to discuss what those terms means and how they can be applied in various public speaking situations.

Final Activity

You're still here?

If you've made it this far in the book, that means you're pretty serious about becoming a better, more skilled presenter.

I'm so proud of you.

Keep up the good work, and do the final activity below.

Directions

How did you feel at the beginning of this book? How do you feel now? Does it seem like you have a solid game plan for being more prepared and confident the next time you are 'onstage'?

Consider how you're feeling right now and do the following.

Watch the TEDx talk: The Skill of Self Confidence by Dr. Ivan Joseph at TEDxRyersonU and take his advice.
Video: https://www.youtube.com/watch?v=w-HYZv6HzAs

There will be times when your confidence might be low, and there will be times when your confidence will be pretty high (savor those times!). Write down those positive moments to reassure yourself when you are not feeling your strongest.

You're going to write a self-confidence letter.

To paraphrase Dr. Joseph's directions: "Write a letter to yourself when you're feeling good." It should be "your own personal brag sheet, about the things you are proud of."

~

Start now, I'll help guide you:

(Your name here),

Congrats on accomplishing _____ *(insert a goal you accomplished).*

I'm so proud of you! Do you remember when you started, how you weren't sure you could do it? You did it.

Congrats on helping that person complete _____ *(insert something you did for someone else). You probably helped them more than you know.*

(I don't know what other small or large things you have accomplished in your life that might have special significance to you, so keep writing in the space below, now that we have the ball rolling!)

~

Bring out this letter and read it as often as you need to.

There may be times when you don't want to, but that's when you need it most. It will help put you back on the right track.

Being on stage can be scary and difficult, and so can gaining the courage and self-confidence to get up there, but I have no doubt you can do it.

Continue to read and reread this short book when you need some help. Share this book with others who may need it just as much as you did (you may want to tear out your "letter to self" before passing it on).

Let the journey continue, and don't forget to always be prepared, feel confident, and have fun.

Sincerely,

Erin Lovell Ebanks
You can contact me at Erin@happyprofessor.com

Share *The 3-Step Speech*

Do you know someone else who is nervous to get up in front of a crowd? Maybe they're struggling with school or sabotaging their career as a result.

Make a list of friends, family members, colleagues, and co-workers who might need help with an upcoming performance or presentation, and then loan this book to as many of them as you can. Have each person cross their name off the list once they've finished:

_____

_____

_____

_____

_____

_____

_____

_____

_____

Please return this book to: _____

Personal notes & insights from *The 3-Step Speech*:

Personal notes & insights from *The 3-Step Speech*:

*Note from the author: Much of the content that I have shared with the readers in *The 3-Step Speech* is a combination of the recollections of the various communication books from my own studies, and my personal years of experience as a public speaker and speech teacher. Any similarities with other books, texts or course materials are simply a matter of my extensive studies in the field of communication and public speaking.

About the Author

Erin Lovell Ebanks is the adjunct professor behind the website happyprofessor.com where she writes about student success, classroom tips, and living life. She teaches a number of online and face-to-face classes each semester, ranging from Introduction to Communication to Family Communication.

At 23, Erin taught her first college course while in grad school, and never looked back. Today, she's still finding new ways to connect with students and make life worthwhile, from spending quite some time in the classroom and most of her free time doing anything outdoors- even if that means grading online assignments outside the local coffee shop.

Erin has a BA in Communication Studies from Stetson University in DeLand, Florida, and an MA in Mass Media Communication from the University of Central Florida in Orlando, Florida.

~

Books by the author:

Happy Professor: An Adjunct Instructor's Guide to Personal, Financial, and Student Success

The 3-Step Speech: How to Build a Message, Feel Confident, and Have Fun